A DAY IN THE LIFE OF
THE BRITISH
ARMY

A DAY IN THE LIFE OF
THE BRITISH
ARMY

COLONEL MICHAEL DEWAR

A DAVID & CHARLES
MILITARY BOOK

Book designed by Michael Head

Typeset by Ace Filmsetting Ltd, Frome, Somerset
and printed in Portugal by Resopal
for David & Charles plc
Brunel House, Newton Abbott, Devon

Distributed in the United States by
Sterling Publishing Co Inc
387 Park Avenue South, New York, NY 10016-8810

Contents

Foreword

Whilst there are innumerable published works on every aspect of military affairs, it struck me as a serving soldier (at the time of writing) that by far the best way to get a real insight into the life, roles, purpose and ethos of the British Army was to take a snapshot of the organisation at a given moment in time. Thus the idea emerged that a day would be chosen at random, and representatives of the Army scattered around the world on that day should be asked to recount their activities. So taken with the idea were the British military authorities that they have co-operated whole-heartedly with the scheme.

I have written a number of books on various military subjects. Many other authors have attempted in one form or another to portray the British Army. None, in my opinion, has succeeded to the same extent as this volume. Perhaps this is because it is a book written by soldiers about soldiers. Two qualities in particular stand out: enthusiasm and professionalism. No matter how obscure, demanding and complex the task, British soldiers have always gone about it in a thoroughly dedicated manner – whether it be peacekeeping for the UN in Namibia, fighting the IRA in Northern Ireland, building a hutted camp in Belize, or simply being put through basic training in the United Kingdom. The British Regular Army is relatively small – approximately 150,000 strong – but it is extraordinarily diverse in its traditions, infrastructure and roles. As a result of the defence cuts announced by the Government in July 1990 it will get even smaller (about 120,000), but its shape and roles will remain largely unchanged. I have tried in this book to capture the spirit of the British Army. That spirit is the same today as it was on 30 June 1989.

MICHAEL DEWAR

Introduction

Strength and deployment

The British Army is about 240,00 strong. That figure includes nearly 157,000 regular soldiers, nearly 73,000 Territorial Army soldiers, the Ulster Defence Regiment which is 6,300 strong, and a Home Service Force which is currently 3,000 strong but scheduled to grow larger in the future. There are some 6,400 women in the Regular Army but this figure is likely to double in the next five years as more women are recruited, not only because of the impending demographic trough of the 1990s, but also because they can do some jobs in the Army as well as, if not better than, their male counterparts. They will, however, be excluded from posts which would involve direct combat with the enemy.

The cuts announced by the Government in July 1990 mean that by 1995 the army will lose some 40,000 troops, mostly from the British Army of the Rhine (BAOR) which will be reduced to one in-theatre division plus some independent units, a total force of some 25,000 compared to its present strength of 55,000. However, the figures in this chapter are valid for the next five years and thereafter it is only the figures for BAOR that will change dramatically.

The Regular Army is stationed, for the most part, in the United Kingdom and Germany. There are about 41,400 regular soldiers in the United Kingdom, although a large proportion of this number – in particular the 2nd Infantry Division in its entirety and the 19th Infantry Brigade – are destined to reinforce BAOR in Germany. Others are likely to be deployed to Denmark (the UK Mobile Force (or UKMF)) or to the flanks of NATO in Norway or Turkey (the Allied Command Europe (or ACE) Mobile Force), leaving only some 30,000 regular soldiers for Home Defence. Together with TA soldiers, reservists, and men and women from the other services, this figure rises to over 100,000. There is still a surprisingly large number of British soldiers stationed elsewhere in the world. There are over 8,000 men in Hong Kong, and at least some of them will remain there until the colony is handed back to the Chinese authorities in 1997. There is also a garrison in Gibraltar, which will be reduced from its present strength of nearly 800 to a token presence in 1991. A Gurkha battalion is stationed in the Sultanate of Brunei by arrangement with the Sultan and at his expense. There is always an infantry battalion group in Belize. As long as there is any vestige of a military threat to Belize from neighbouring Guatemala, the British government has agreed to station an infantry battalion supported by a troop of armoured reconnaissance vehicles, a Blowpipe missile detachment, an artillery battery, some engineers, helicopters and Harrier aircraft there. British forces Cyprus consist of over 3,000 troops, half of whom

Infantrymen on exercise in the UK. The soldier in the foreground carries an 84mm Carl Gustav Medium Anti-tank Weapon or MAW. His team-mate carries the new 5.56 mm Light Support Weapon or LSW. They are also wearing the new British Army helmet introduced in 1986

belong to UNFICYP – the United Nations Forces in Cyprus – whilst the remainder are employed defending the Sovereign Base Areas. When Cyprus gained its independence from Britain in 1960, two areas around Episcopi and Dhekelia, both on the south coast, were retained by Britain for the purpose of stationing troops. The exact size of the garrison in the Falkland Islands and South Georgia is classified but it includes infantry, air defence assets, Phantom interceptor aircraft, naval surface vessels and submarines and other supporting troops. They are likely to remain there for the foreseeable future. British troops in relatively small numbers form part of UN peacekeeping contingents in various parts of the world and also provide training missions in several other countries. In addition there is a continual programme of overseas training in Canada, the United States, Germany, Portugal, the Caribbean and elsewhere.

Organisation

The day-to-day management of the Army is the responsibility of the Army Board, headed by the Chief of the General Staff. There are two major subsidiary headquarters and a number of smaller headquarters worldwide which are controlled from the Ministry of Defence (MoD) thus:

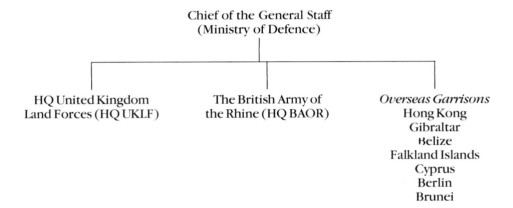

Chief of the General Staff
(Ministry of Defence)

| HQ United Kingdom Land Forces (HQ UKLF) | The British Army of the Rhine (HQ BAOR) | *Overseas Garrisons* Hong Kong Gibraltar Belize Falkland Islands Cyprus Berlin Brunei |

UKLF

HQ UKLF commands the majority of troops in the United Kingdom and, in the event of war, it would be responsible for Home Defence, the reinforcement of BAOR and the NATO flanks, the mobilisation of the Territorial Army (TA) and the reserves and, if necessary, the recruitment and training of further manpower. HQ UKLF commands ten military districts throughout the country. These headquarters would become the regional military headquarters responsible for Home Defence in war. The only formed division in the United Kingdom is the 2nd Infantry Division, which is UKLF's major contribution to the reinforcement of Europe on mobilisation. The division, which is based in York, consist of three brigades, one of which is a regular brigade and the other two of which are Territorial Army Brigades. However, 19 Infantry Brigade also reinforces BAOR, 1 Infantry Brigade reinforces Denmark, and the British contribution to the Allied Command Europe Mobile Force is tasked to reinforce the flanks of NATO, probably Norway or Turkey.

BAOR

The British Army of the Rhine (BAOR) numbers some 55,000 soldiers and is supported by Royal Air Force Germany which has 10,000 men, thirteen squadrons of combat aircraft and two squadrons of helicopters. BAOR is assigned to NATO forces in Western Europe and the Commander-in-Chief BAOR is also Commander of NATO's Northern Army Group (NORTHAG) consisting of the 1st British Corps, the 1st Netherlands Corps, the 1st Belgian Corps, the 1st German Corps and the 3rd US Corps. The latter is stationed in Fort Hood, Texas, and would be deployed to Germany during a period of tension.

NORTHAG is one of two Army Groups responsible for the defence of the Federal Republic of Germany. The other, the Central Army Group or CENTAG, looks after the southern half of Germany. Both Army Groups are commanded by HQ Allied Forces Central Europe (HQ AFCENT) which is responsible for the defence of West Germany, Holland and Belgium. Whilst HQ AFNORTH looks after Norway, Denmark and the Baltic, HQ AFSOUTH

British ski troops on exercise in Norway. Note that they are using cross-country skis for easy movement over long distances. They are carrying on their backs (their backpacks will weigh up to 75lb) or on a sledge all that they need to operate and survive. Britain's Commando Brigade and its Army battalion-strength contribution to the Allied Mobile Force (Land) train in Norway on a regular basis

commands the NATO region incorporating Greece, Italy, Turkey and the Mediterranean.

The 1st British Corps is the main fighting formation of BAOR. The Corps takes its place in the line shoulder to shoulder with the other NATO Corps. It consists of three armoured divisions stationed in Germany and the 2nd Infantry Division which, although it is part of the 1st British Corps' order of battle, is based in York. Each of the armoured divisions differs slightly, but their basic organisation is:

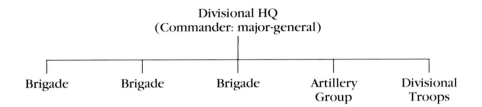

Brigades in 1st British Corps are all armoured brigades. Again they vary in organisation and can consist of a different mix of three or four major units, but the usual organisation of an armoured brigade in Germany is:

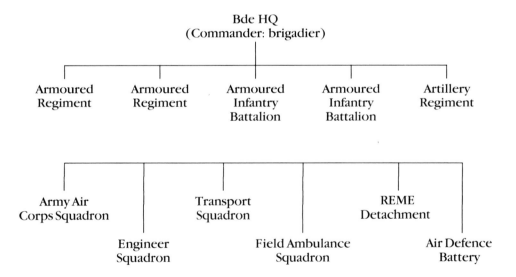

Brigades are further subdivided into smaller formations known as battlegroups, which are the basic building bricks of the brigades and divisions. A battlegroup is commanded by a lieutenant-colonel whose infantry battalion or armoured regiment provides the command and staff element of the battlegroup, which is then structured according to its task into the correct mix of armour, infantry and supporting arms. For instance, a battlegroup which has been tasked to mount an armoured attack across open German heathland will probably be 'armour heavy' with two tank squadrons and perhaps only one infantry company. This is because speed and armoured shock action will be necessary for success. Therefore infantry in this situation are less important. If on the other hand a battlegroup is tasked to clear a built-up area or advance through a forested area, it is likely to be 'infantry heavy', because it will be necessary to clear close country with infantry first to avoid tanks being ambushed at close quarters. Thus the battlegroup's organisation is very flexible and the infantry companies or armoured squadrons can be quickly regrouped to cope with a change in the threat. A typical battlegroup fighting a defence battle and based upon an organisation of the armoured squadron and two armoured infantry companies could contain about six hundred men, sixteen tanks and about eighty mechanised combat vehicles (MCVs) and armoured personnel carriers (APCs). The tank will be the Challenger MBT and the MCV the new Warrior.

Similarly the commanding officer of a battlegroup will 'mix and match' his armoured and infantry assets into three combat teams or company groups. These will consist of perhaps one troop of tanks and two platoons of infantry, with supporting elements depending on the task.

Berlin

The Berlin Garrison of approximately 3,000 men is a force separate from and not under the command of HQ 1st British Corps. It consists of three infantry battalions, an armoured squadron and a number of minor units. It is part of an Allied force put in place to occupy and garrison the former German capital at the end of the Second World War. The other three occupying powers are the United States, the Soviet Union and France. For almost thirty-five years, Berlin was an island of the West in the middle of Communist East Germany, its garrison being there to uphold western rights in West Berlin and, if necessary, fight to defend the city. Although the situation in Berlin is changing rapidly, the four-power status of Berlin is unlikely to be affected in the immediate future, and certainly not until Soviet forces have been withdrawn from what is at the time of writing still East Germany.

Northern Ireland

The military presence in support of the civilian authorities in Ulster is controlled by HQ Northern Ireland which is located at Lisburn just outside Belfast. HQ Northern Ireland has three brigades under its command, stationed in Belfast, Londonderry and South Armagh. These brigades consist of a mixture of resident battalions on a standard two-year tour, and so-called 'Roulement' battalions which are rotated through the province from BAOR and UKLF for shorter six-month tours. Also forming part of these brigades are the battalions of the Ulster Defence Regiment, or UDR, a force raised for internal security duties in the province. It is 6,300 strong, of which about 3,700 are part-time soldiers.

Reserve forces

Every officer and soldier completing a regular engagement in the Army has a liability for reserve service. Length of service on the reserve varies, but a typical enlistment contract would commit a soldier to a term of 9/22 years. This means he is committed to serve nine years' service as a regular, and the remaining thirteen on the Regular Army reserve. Officers remain on the reserve list until they are fifty-five years old.

On mobilisation the approximately 150,000 men and women who are at present on the reserve would be recalled for service. However, many of them would have left the Regular Army some time previously, and it is generally acknowledged that someone who has been out of the Army for five years or more would not be fit for front line duty. Equipment and procedures change fast and they would not be able to cope without retraining. However, a minimal amount of training of reservists does take place. In order to qualify for a small annual bounty a reservist must make a brief appearance at a nominated army training establishment on an annual basis. During the few hours he is there he must undertake some basic form of training, like firing a rifle or fitting his gas mask. Approximately 75,000 men and women have left the Army in the past five years and it is these reservists who would probably be used to bring front line units up to war establishment.

The Territorial Army is currently reaching the end of an expansion programme. It is so called because it was – and is – recruited on a county or local basis: it was the successor to the Volunteer Force and was formed in 1908,

A Scorpion reconnaissance vehicle (foreground) and a Scimitar on patrol in Norway during NATO exercises. The Scorpion mounts a 76mm gun whilst the Scimitar, similar in every other respect, mounts a 30mm Rarden cannon

taking a prominent part in both World Wars. The TA is a national reserve designed to reinforce the Regular Army in an emergency. Today it would provide some 30 per cent of the Army's total strength in war and over 50 per cent of Home Defence forces. Nevertheless it consumes only about 5 per cent of the Army budget.

The most recently formed part of the TA is the Home Service Force. The idea received considerable publicity when it was first made public in 1980. It inevitably attracted such epithets as 'Dad's Army', but in fact it bears little or no resemblance to the Home Guard of the Second World War. It began as a pilot scheme of only four companies in 1982 and, because of the initial success of the scheme, the decision was taken to expand the force to a total of forty-seven companies by 1990.

On mobilisation the TA would add some forty infantry battalions, four armoured reconnaissance regiments, three parachute battalions, two SAS regiments, eleven signal regiments, seven engineer regiments, two field artillery regiments and three air defence regiments to the Regular Army's order of battle. Its contribution is therefore immensely important. Indeed, the July 1990 defence announcement emphasised the continuing importance of the TA.

This anti-tank team is armed with an 84mm Carl Gustav medium anti-tank gun (right) and the SA-80 5.56mm rifle

Tank forces

There are nineteen Regular armoured regiments and five TA armoured regiments in the British Army. Collectively they are known as the Royal Armoured Corps (RAC). There are currently eleven Regular armoured regiments serving in BAOR, equipped with either Chieftain or Challenger main battle tanks (MBTs) and two armoured reconnaissance regiments equipped with Scorpion and Scimitar recce vehicles. In the UK there are three further Regular armoured regiments with MBTs, which mostly have a training role in peacetime. There are also three Regular armoured reconnaissance regiments stationed in the UK. The five TA yeomanry regiments provide two armoured recce regiments for the reinforcement of BAOR and three for home defence. By 1995 the RAC is likely to be smaller by up to five armoured regiments.

The tank fleet presently consists of Challenger 1 and ageing Chieftain tanks. Chieftain is becoming increasingly unreliable and is due to be replaced from the early 1990s by a new tank which is to be selected from the British Challenger 2, the West German Leopard 2, or the US M1A2 Abrams, all of which compare favourably with the Soviet T-80. The supremacy of the tank, which has a cross-country speed of perhaps fifty or sixty kph and an effective gun range of 2,000 metres, is being challenged on the battlefield by attack helicopters such as the Soviet Hind and the US Apache, which travel at speeds of up to 300 kph and carry up to sixteen missiles with ranges of 4,000 metres. However, helicopters are also vulnerable to air defence weapons, to other helicopters and to weather. There will be room for both tanks and helicopters on the battlefield for the foreseeable future.

The Challenger is armed with a 120 mm rifled gun and is powered by a Rolls-Royce CV12 engine which generates 1,200 bhp at 2,300 rpm. Its maximum road speed is 56 kph and it weighs 62 tonnes. A particular feature is its Chobham armour, the exact composition of which is classified but which is known to be a form of sandwich armour.

The Infantry

The British infantry is fifty-five battalions strong: by 1995 it is likely to lose up to eight of these. These battalions are generally, though not always, formed into large regiments which consist of two or more battalions, and which come under the command of a Division of Infantry. The Division of Infantry is a peacetime administrative organisation and should not be confused with operational formations such as the 1st, 3rd and 4th Divisions in BAOR and the 2nd Infantry Division in UKLF. The Divisions of Infantry are:

> The Guards Division – 8 battalions
> The Scottish Division – 7 battalions
> The Queen's Division – 9 battalions
> The King's Division – 8 battalions
> The Prince of Wales's Division – 9 battalions
> The Light Division – 6 battalions

The Parachute Regiment (three battalions) and the Brigade of Gurkhas (five battalions) are not part of a Division. With the exception of the Guards Divi-

Training in Cyprus. The soldier's SA-80 Rifle has been fitted with a blank-firing attachment which ensures that the weapon is recocked after firing each shot. It also prevents the 'wadding' from a blank round injuring an opponent at close range

sion and the Brigade of Gurkhas, all these divisions have a varying number of the forty TA infantry battalions under their administrative control.

Armoured infantry battalions in BAOR will all soon be equipped with the Warrior MCV. It is armed with the 30 mm Rarden Cannon, which is a good anti-APC weapon up to a range of about 1,500 metres, and a Hughes Chain gun. The Warrior can carry ten men, of whom two are crew. The introduction of this vehicle into the 1st (British) Corps will enable the infantry to keep up with the tank on the battlefield. Some reinforcing battalions are equipped with the wheeled Saxon APC, a much more basic vehicle designed to transport twelve men on the battlefield in relative safety. It is not, like the Warrior, designed to fight from.

The infantry, more often than not, will fight on its feet. In the case of airmobile battalions this will always be the case. Each rifleman has recently been issued with a new 5.56 mm personal weapon, the SA80, and each fireteam of four men with a Light Support Weapon (LSW). In addition the infantry is equipped with 81 mm mortars, the LAW 80 anti-tank weapon, the Milan anti-tank missile, the General Purpose Machine Gun (GPMG) and the 51 mm light mortar.

The Artillery

The Royal Artillery provides the battlefield fire support and air defence for the Army in the field. Its various regiments are equipped so as to provide close fire support using light and medium guns, battlefield nuclear support using missiles and guns, area and point air defence using missiles, and lastly various specialised artillery locating tasks. The strength of the artillery in UKLF is:

3 Field Regiments
1 Commando Field Regiment
1 Parachute Field Regiment
1 Air Defence Regiment (Rapier)
1 Locating Regiment
2 TA Field Regiments
4 TA Air Defence Regiments (Blowpipe and Javelin)
Artillery School Support Regiment

In BAOR there are:

8 Field Regiments (Abbot or M109)
1 Heavy Regiment (MLRS)
2 Missile Regiments (Lance)
2 Heavy Regiments (MLRS and locating capability)
2 Air Defence Regiments (Rapier)

This total is bound to be affected when BAOR is reorganised.

Combat teams in a battlegroup will each have a forward observation officer (FOO) with them. His job is to direct the fire of the close support battalions' guns on to the target. He is in direct radio contact with the gun position. Having identified the target, the FOO will call for fire from the guns and he will

then adjust the fall of shot to cover the target area. He may use a laser rangefinder for calculating the precise range to the target. Other computer systems enable the guns to locate themselves precisely and to calculate other data such as wind speed, type of ammunition, barrel wear and other weapon variables that will affect the fall of shot.

Infantrymen on manoeuvres in the Falkland Islands. The loads they are carrying are similar to those carried by British Forces across the Falklands during the repossession of the islands in 1982

All these supporting systems not only provide very accurate fire but, more importantly, allow FOOs to direct a large number of guns on to one target and then switch them to another quickly and accurately. Modern artillery fire can be moved about the battlefield with astonishing efficiency.

The Royal Artillery is equipped with the 155 mm M109 and 105 mm Abbot self-propelled guns for close support. The M109 also has a nuclear capability. The Multi-Launch Rocket System (MLRS) is now being introduced into the Royal Artillery. It fires a batch of six 227 mm rockets over 30,000 metres. The rockets either have conventional HE warheads, or they can carry 600 M42 minelets or anti-tank sub-munitions. It is a devastating system which will add immeasurably to the strength of the Royal Artillery. The missile regiment is armed with twelve Lance missile launchers, each capable of projecting a nuclear warhead 120 km. The two Air Defence Regiments in BAOR are equipped with tracked Rapier, a highly effective area air defence system with a range of 6,800 metres.

In UKLF, artillery is towed. The main weapon systems are the FH70 howitzer, a 155 mm gun with a range of 24 kilometres, and the 105 mm Light Gun which has a maximum range of 17.2 kilometres. Both are excellent guns. The Light Gun proved itself in the Falklands War, where it was flown into action by Sea King helicopters.

Javelin is the British Army's successor to Blowpipe and it is already in service in BAOR and UKLF. It is an electronically more sophisticated system, with a greater range and a night sight. All that the operator has to do is keep the aiming mark on the target, leaving the guidance system to do the rest. It is man-portable and has a maximum range of five kilometres.

The Royal Artillery is also responsible for operating Midge drones for battle-field surveillance, ZB298 battlefield radars, sound ranging equipment, meteorological equipment and Cymbeline mortar locating radar. Gunners have to be jacks of all trades!

The Army Air Corps

The Army Air Corps consists of four separate regiments, three of which are stationed in Germany with BAOR, and a number of independent squadrons. About 300 AAC helicopters are used for anti-tank operations, artillery fire control, reconnaissance, liaison flying and, occasionally, for troop lifting. Most troop lifting is undertaken by the RAF, which operates about 180 Puma and Chinook helicopters for this purpose.

The helicopter is fast becoming as important a weapon system on the battle-field as the tank. The Soviets have invested vast sums of money in the Hind attack helicopter, as have the Americans with the Apache. Both these aircraft are purpose-built attack helicopters incorporating missile, rocket and gun systems. Although the British Army's attack helicopter was not purpose-built, the Westland Lynx helicopter armed with the TOW anti-tank missile is nevertheless an extremely effective system. The Lynx is a fast and agile helicopter and it can mount eight TOW missiles, which have a range of 4,000 metres. It can carry a further eight missiles as a reload. The combination of the TOW missile and Lynx helicopter make a very effective tank killing system.

The AAC is also equipped with the Scout helicopter which, although somewhat long in the tooth – it has been flown by the AAC since 1962 – is still a rugged and effective utility helicopter. However, the main general purpose and reconnaissance helicopter used by the AAC is the Gazelle. This is a French designed helicopter built under licence by Westland. Normally these are not armed, though they were fitted with rockets in the Falklands conflict.

The Royal Engineers

The Royal Engineers provide specialist support to the combat formations, such as mine clearance, mine laying, route construction, demolition, bridge building, ditching, map making, water supply, bomb disposal, building and airfield construction and repair, postal services, and even underwater reconnaissance. In BAOR there are five engineer regiments as well as one armoured engineer regiment and one amphibious engineer regiment. The former provides minefield breaching support in the shape of armoured vehicles Royal Engineers (AVREs), Combat Engineer Tractors (CETs) and armoured bridge laying equipment. The latter is equipped with the M2 floating bridge. In a nutshell Engineers are in the business of improving mobility for our own formations and reducing the mobility (counter-mobility) of the enemy.

In UKLF the Engineers have four regular regiments and seven TA regiments, all of which are capable of reinforcing BAOR. There are also a number of independent squadrons in UKLF.

The Engineers are equipped with a myriad of complex equipment. This varies from a range of different kinds of anti-tank and anti-personnel mines, to equipment such as the Giant Viper, which is a system for clearing lanes through a minefield. It consists of a hose which is filled with explosive and attached to a large rocket. The whole equipment is mounted on a trailer and towed by an AVRE. The trailer is positioned near the 'home' edge of a minefield and the rocket fired, dumping the explosive-filled hose across the minefield. The subsequent explosion of the hose will clear a lane wide enough for a tank to drive through.

The Royal Signals

The Royal Corps of Signals provide the communications throughout the command system of the Army. Individual battlegroups are responsible for providing their own internal communications, but all communications from brigade level and above are the responsibility of the Royal Signals. They operate systems ranging from field telephones linked by wire, through point-to-point microwave radio systems, VHF and HF radios, and battlefield computer systems, to secure communications using satellites (SATCOM).

The Royal Signals operate the new Ptarmigan secure battlefield communications system that links battlefield formations in a grid system. It has built-in redundancy so that if parts of the system are damaged, calls are automatically re-routed. Ptarmigan can also be used to carry information processed by the Army's battlefield computer system, called Wavell. This system is designed to accept information from all the battlefield intelligence agencies and produce the information down to brigade level on a VDU or in hard copy.

Combat support

The so-called 'Teeth' Arms cannot operate for extended periods unless they are supplied with fuel, ammunition and rations, and unless men and equipment are replaced or repaired. These services are provided by the Royal Corps of Transport (RCT), the Royal Army Ordnance Corps (RAOC), the Royal Electrical and Mechanical Engineers (REME) and the Royal Army Medical Corps (RAMC). Soldiers in these vital logistic units represent about fifteen per cent of the manpower of an armoured division.

The RCT is responsible for transporting the vast tonnages of combat supplies (ammunition, fuel and rations) that are required by an army in the field. The RAOC on the other hand holds, stores and issues all these items. The REME mends them when they go wrong, or recovers them when they break down. Soldiers also need repair and recovery when they are wounded in battle. This is the job of the RAMC, which is responsible for the health of the British Army in peace and war.

Other needs of the army are met by:

- The Intelligence Corps – advises on security and intelligence matters.
- The Army Catering Corps (ACC) – provides the trained cooks that serve throughout the Army.

- The Royal Pioneer Corps (RPC) – provides fighting soldiers who are trained to assist in the movement of stores and in other manpower intensive duties.
- The Royal Army Educational Corps (RAEC) – consists of an all-officer corps responsible for the education of officers and soldiers.
- The Royal Army Veterinary Corps (RAVC) – looks after the many animals in the Army.
- The Army Physical Training Corps (APTC) – consists of officers and mainly SNCOs, who are responsible for army fitness.
- The Royal Military Police (RMP) – responsible for discipline, traffic control and crime prevention.
- The Royal Army Chaplain's Department (RAChD) – provides chaplains for the five major religious denominations.
- The Royal Army Pay Corps (RAPC) – responsible for financial services throughout the army.
- The Women's Royal Army Corps (WRAC) – provides over 5,000 women who serve with almost every branch of the army.
- The Queen Alexandra's Royal Army Nursing Corps (QARANC) – provides the nurses for army hospitals.

The revolution that took place in Europe in late 1989, and which shows no signs of abating, will undoubtedly bring with it major changes for the British Army. Some troops will be withdrawn from Europe, the Army will certainly be reduced in strength but its spirit will remain undaunted, its tasks for the most part unchanged and it will face the future with the same determination as it has always done. The following chapters are a snapshot of the British Army on 30 June 1989.

An anti-tank gunner running to his firing position. This photograph was taken on a live firing range at Senneybridge in Wales. Soldiers train in realistic conditions using live ammunition

Britain

Exercise Roaring Lion:
5 Airborne Brigade

Captain R J Metcalfe

5 Airborne Brigade is the Army's 'Instant Readiness' Force, and is able to deploy anywhere in the world in a matter of days. Here we see it practising for just this role.

On the island of Safra (Salisbury Plain training area) the situation has become desperate. The ruling royal family have been embezzling oil revenues and have been ousted from power by the Safran Peoples' Liberation Party. This presents the powerful neighbouring country of Guambia with the opportunity to invade the island, under the pretext of a request for assistance from the royal family. Guambia's historical claim on the island has become more significant since oil was discovered, and the main reason for the invasion is economic.

A private from I Para, 5 Airborne Brigade, with his face camouflaged ready for Exercise Roaring Lion

Safra has a defence agreement with the UK, and Her Majesty's Government is obliged to deploy military force to assist in restoring the island's independence. 5 Airborne Brigade has been tasked to carry out the mission, as the Army's only dedicated force earmarked for operations outside the NATO area.

Guambian forces on the ground are currently occupying defensive positions to the west of the vital oil installations, which are situated in the northeast of the island. They are reinforcing all the time by both air and sea. They have an airborne capability (1 PARA) which was used to secure their early objectives by parachute assault. Their intention is assessed as being to seize the oil installations at the earliest opportunity. It is therefore vital that UK forces deploy to Safra as soon as possible.

At RAF Lyneham 500 men are sweating over the vast amounts of equipment the individual soldier attaches to his body prior to jumping into a theatre of war. Many men will leave the aircraft with weights not far short of their own body weight; almost all of this kit will be essential to carry out the soldiers' tasks. It will include the personal weapon, three days' rations and ammunition, along with as much water as can be carried, and also nuclear, biological and chemical warfare equipment, since the enemy is known to have a chemical weapons capability. It may include parts of larger support weapons such as mortars, radio equipment and spare batteries. It will almost certainly include little or no personal equipment, as there simply is not enough space. The comforts of home will be in short supply.

In an hour's time the men will board a crowded, and today extremely hot, C-130 Hercules aircraft. They will fly at low level for two hours, with many men suffering the effects of air sickness and dehydration. In spite of the inevitable tension, it will be a relief to jump out of the aircraft. The men have been exhaustively briefed on drop zones and emergency procedures, as well as the ground plan, to the extent that any man or unit should be able to carry out another's task. However, they have not been briefed that in this case the drop zone will be changed at the last minute. A few men will not get the message during the flight, and will land believing themselves to be on a different drop zone. Confusion is inevitable. The aim of this is to test the flexibility of every man in the group by imposing a situation which requires a major change in the plan, at no notice. The men in the group will have to cope with this sudden change of plan as if they had known about it all along.

This group is the leading parachute battalion group, or LPBG. It is self-sustaining for three days, and includes all the men, equipment and stores required to fight in a limited conflict. In this case it is based on the Parachute Regiment's 2nd Battalion (2 PARA), supported by light armoured vehicles of the Life Guards, gunners from 7 Parachute Regiment Royal Horse Artillery (7 PARA RHA), engineers from 9 Parachute Squadron (9 PARA SQN RE), medics from 23 Parachute Field Ambulance (23 PFA), and the many other essential elements which have grouped with the LPBG for this particular exercise. Such grouping is always tailored to suit the requirements of the specific operation or exercise. Later in the day it will take less than five minutes simultaneously to drop the whole group, with their stores, into Safra from fifteen C-130 Hercules aircraft.

The technique used for jumping in these numbers is known as static line

The drop into SAFRA begins

parachuting. This means that the parachute release is attached to the aircraft by a line which automatically opens the parachute on exiting the aircraft. The man is also equipped with a reserve parachute and a container for his personal equipment. This container is fitted to one of the man's legs shortly before the drop, and is lowered from the body on a rope once the parachutist has left the aircraft. This allows it to land nearby but not interfere with the descent. Using this method a full C-130 Hercules aircraft load of ninety heavily-laden troops can be dispatched from two parallel side doors in no more than forty-five seconds. The drop is from 800 feet, giving an individual time of descent of about forty seconds, depending on individual weights. A total of 1,280 soldiers will be deployed this way during the course of the exercise. This will be immediately preceded by the dispatch from the tail-gate of the aircraft of a 'wedge', a platform containing up to a ton of stores. In addition to this, stores may be dropped as 'door bundles' from the side doors. Vehicles are loaded on to special platforms and dropped out of aircraft specifically designated to carry out this task on to adjacent or parallel drop zones.

At the same time, elements of the 1st Battalion the Royal Regiment of Fusi-

Parachutists from 5 Airborne Brigade land on Salisbury Plain

liers (1 RFF), one of two non-parachute-trained battalions in the brigade, are also preparing for an airborne operation. In this instance one hundred men, with two Scorpion armoured vehicles and two stripped-down Land-Rovers, will be landed on and seize an airfield held by a small enemy force. The aircraft will land, disgorge the troops and take off again immediately, being on the ground for less than three minutes. This operation will coincide with the parachute landings 'up country'. Securing this airfield is vital to the success of the operation, because much of the remainder of the brigade will land by aircraft later.

The remaining infantry unit in the brigade is the 1st Battalion 2nd King Edward VII's Own Gurkhas (1/2 GR). It is also preparing to take off for Safra, to be moved straight into a defensive position by Chinook and Puma support helicopters. Under these circumstances the Chinook can carry up to fifty fully-equipped men, and the Puma carries sixteen. The battalion group will be complete in Safra by early evening.

Almost all of these elements depend in some way for their initial success on the brigade's own advanced forces, the Pathfinder Platoon. This small unit,

27

consisting of highly-skilled soldiers recruited from within the brigade, jumped into Safra in the early hours of this morning. The method they employed for the drop is known as HALO (high altitude low opening). The Pathfinder Platoon is the only brigade sub-unit to use this free-fall technique, which enhances the chances of avoiding detection and involves leaving the aircraft at heights of up to 25,000 feet, followed by a long free-fall descent and then landing using steerable parachutes. Their tasks on landing are to check the drop zones and landing sites for enemy activity, and mark them for the incoming aircraft, as well as performing detailed reconnaissance tasks of key targets and objectives. They will meet up with the commanding officers of some of the major units on the ground to brief them on the results of their reconnaissance. Later in the day they will be rebriefed to move well forward of the remainder of the brigade, to carry out further intelligence-gathering activities.

At the end of Day One there are well over 2,000 soldiers in Safra, all of whom have arrived by air transport. Many more are awaiting follow-on air-land sorties, along with the large numbers of vehicles and stores that were not delivered with the initial assaults. However, not all of the necessary supporting organisations, personnel, equipment and stores can be transported by air, and must therefore sail to Safra. This 'sea tail' left Marchwood today aboard the logistic landing ship (LSL) *Sir Galahad*. In due course they will arrive in Safra to be offloaded over a beach and thence travel by road into the theatre of operations. Until then, resupply to the front line units will be by airdrop (parachute) resupply. In all, over 300 tons of stores will be delivered into Safra this way, with individual aircraft capable of dispatching up to twenty-four one-ton containers per sortie.

The situation in Safra itself has continued to deteriorate, with enemy forces now in a position to press home attacks against the vital areas. Defensive positions must be prepared as fast as possible. In particular the positions around the vital bridges across the river lying between the oilfields and the enemy must be secured. This is quickly achieved by 2 PARA and 1 RRF, although the enemy have already destroyed one of the bridges. The Life Guards and the Pathfinder Platoon push out a reconnaissance screen to the front of the bridges and give early warning of the inevitable enemy attacks which occur during the night. The Gurkhas occupy a depth position around the oilfields. They too will be attacked by an enemy force (1 PARA), parachuted into friendly forces' positions with a view to causing maximum confusion. This attack will coincide with heliborne assaults to attack friendly forces' positions from an unexpected direction.

At the end of the first day 5 Airborne Brigade has achieved its objectives. If all goes according to plan the enemy will fall back into a defensive position to the west of the area, around an airfield. The brigade will force them to withdraw most of their forces and will defeat the remainder in a classic set-piece brigade attack, on a well-sited defensive position. Prior to this, parachute and heliborne raiding tasks will take place on pockets of enemy around Safra and on adjacent islands (other training areas). Logistic units will be established well forward, with resupply aircraft landing on 'dirt strips', which in reality are no more than flat fields. Finally, British forces will be withdrawn once the

The C-130 Hercules disappearing into the gloom has just deposited these parachutists of the Parachute Brigade on to the ground. They exited from the aircraft at a height of approximately 800ft. The bundles hanging underneath each parachutist contain their equipment. The fact that it hits the ground before its owner lessens the impact for the parachutist.

territorial integrity of the island has been restored. This will be by helicopter and Hercules aircraft, taking less than half a day for the majority of the fighting troops.

Day One of the exercise is over. Clearly it has not been a typical day, even for 5 Airborne Brigade; yet such operations have taken place seventy-three times since the Second World War. The benefits of training days such as today will be fully realised when a similar situation arises in the future, as it inevitably will.

The Army Physical Training Corps

Captain J V Larkham APTC

The Army Physical Training Corps is responsible for keeping the Army fit. At its HQ in Aldershot it runs various PT courses and trains instructors who are then sent world-wide to maintain standards of fitness in every unit of the British Army.

The best way to illustrate a typical day in the life of the Corps is to see what one man, in this case Warrant Officer Class 2(WO2) C Wilkinson, did on 30 June 1989.

He arrived for work at the Army School of Physical Training at 0730 hours. At 0810 he gathered his staff around him for the daily conference to discuss the day ahead, before taking the morning parade of those attending various courses at the school, to ensure that everyone had turned up for work. He was then required to go down to the ranges to practise shooting with the 9 mm pistol. PTIs may spend most of their life in gymnasia, but they are first and foremost soldiers, and are expected to keep up their military skills.

After an extremely quick change from combat kit to PT order, he was taking

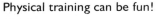

Physical training can be fun!

an anatomy class by 1100 hours. After another quick change he spent the lunch-hour bicycling around Aldershot at high speed, training for a triathlon event later in the summer. The afternoon was spent in the Aldershot Military Athletics Stadium officiating as a starter. At 1600 hours WO2 Wilkinson gave some treatment to a fellow PTI who had injured his back in the gymnasium trying to show off! Being a qualified physiotherapist and a PTI can be a useful combination. Finally he spent an hour from 1630 to 1730 in his office finishing off his paperwork and checking on the next day's programme. But, as is so often the case in the Army, that was not the end of the day: from 1930 to 2130 that evening he had agreed to referee a boxing competition between two local regiments. Friday 30 June was not untypical of a normal day at the PT School. The motto of the APTC is 'A Healthy Mind in a Healthy Body', but there is no doubt that a sense of humour also helps!

Boxing is a popular sport in the Army. Here WO2 Wilkinson referees a match in the gymnasium in Aldershot

Pairs Obs and Recce: 7 Regiment, Army Air Corps

Captain Darrell Locke AAC

The Army Air Corps flies all the Army's helicopters. Here Captain Darrell Locke describes what he did on 30 June 1989.

0930 on a Friday morning and I'm about to start work. Normally this might earn me an interview without coffee with my Flight Commander, but I do have an excuse for arriving at work an hour later than usual – Gazelle Flight were night-flying last night.

Flying at any time of the day is demanding; at night the demands can be greater, but they are far outweighed by the privilege of seeing the earth from such a spectacular vantage point. Whether it is flying through the valleys of Norway in a landscape lit only by the dim glow of the snow-covered mountains, or across the almost solid darkness of Salisbury Plain, you can't beat flying with the owls and the bats. Anyone with the slightest interest in aviation will know of the array of technical devices which enable a pilot to navigate himself and his aircraft with pinpoint accuracy around the globe. In the Army, however, we draw lines on our maps and off we go. There is no sense in training to use fancy navigation aids when we would be unable to use them in wartime, and besides – that's cheating. This all sounds well and good until you find yourself airborne at night, armed only with a line on a map, and you find that none of the features on your map can be seen because – surprise, surprise – it's dark! That's not strictly true, of course; roads and buildings stand out because of the lights which people kindly leave on for us. So we navigate at night by relating built-up areas to the map and using time and distance – flying on a known heading for a known time. Sometimes, like last night, if we are landing in a field location we will be able to home-in on radio transmissions from a ground station and fly until we are overhead. Then it is a relatively simple matter to descend and land in the field, though it can be fun when the only thing visible in the black outside the cockpit is the light of the marshaller's torch (just try judging how far away a solitary light is when you are next out on a moonless night).

At least night flying has earned us an extra hour in bed. No such luxury for the four members of Scout Flight, who have been out flying since before 0400. The Paras have been jumping into one of the dropping zones on Salisbury Plain since first light, so the Scouts have been on standby on the DZ in case there should be any casualties. Luckily they are more likely to be used to collect the used parachutes scattered across the DZ.

As well as the Gazelle and Scout helicopters of 658 Squadron, 7 Regiment Army Air Corps comprises 656 Squadron with a flight of Gazelles and one of Lynx anti-tank helicopters, and 2 Flight with their six Gazelles. The Aerospatiale Gazelle forms a large part of the Regiment and thus is the real workhorse. In peacetime the Gazelle earns its living on such tasks as ferrying VIPs around the country. When not involved in tasking, we train for our wartime roles such as observation and reconnaissance, or Air Observation Post work. On top of all this the pilots need to reach certain training levels, for example night or instrument flying, thus enabling us to fly twenty-four hours a day and in poor weather.

Most Army helicopters now operate with a crew of two, and the Gazelles of 658 Squadron are no exception. The pilot in the left-hand seat will command the aircraft and make all the tactical decisions, leaving the other pilot to concentrate on flying safely. Command of the aircraft rests with the more experienced pilot, rather than the one of higher rank, so that the situation can arise where a recently promoted sergeant is making the tactical decisions for a relatively senior captain.

This morning we are going to carry out what we call a 'pairs obs and recce'

Infantrymen are ferried forward to their positions during an exercise in Berlin. This is an unusual task for a Gazelle helicopter which is normally used for reconnaissance duties

Lynx helicopters of the Army
Air Corps take off

task. Two Gazelles will go out together and find vantage points from which to observe notional enemy positions. Each aircraft will be acting as an extra set of eyes for the other in an attempt to see before being seen. For our training purposes we will be presented with a tactical scenario together with a target to try to observe. This target may be a building or a crossroads, or even an airfield, depending on how devious the compiler of the exercise has been.

While the two aircraft commanders get their heads together to sort out the best approach to the problem we have been set, the two pilots sort out the flying side of life. What is the weather like? Which aircraft have we got and can it take two crew and a full load of fuel? Are there any Royal flights on today, or any other airspace restrictions? Well, it looks as though the Queen Mother is off to Scotland for the day, but that won't affect us, so it seems that we can go ahead.

Returning to the operations and planning room, our aircraft commanders are briefed on factors likely to affect the sortie, and then it's into the tactical briefing.

'Enemy forward elements are believed to have reached this road. Our mission is to find out how far they have advanced and in which direction they are

heading. Guns are available.' This last comment doesn't mean that we can strap on our sixshooters and holsters, but rather the guns of the artillery are on call if we should have a chance to use them. The Gazelle has no armament of its own, so uses the firepower of the artillery and of fighter ground attack aircraft, if available. We direct aircraft or gunfire on to their targets for maximum accuracy. Of course today there are no real guns – only a radio ground station playing the role to give us practice in procedures.

Briefing completed, pilots head for the aircraft while aircraft commanders complete the last-minute documentation. Now just kick the tyres, light the fires and leap off unarmed into battle. Well, it's not quite like that in real life, more a case of methodical checks to minimise any possible risks; firstly, the exterior of the aircraft, then all the internal switches, knobs, buttons and dials. When all is checked we start engine and rotors. We are cleared by Air Traffic Control to taxi and take off. Once clear of Salisbury Plain the real flying begins. Our aircraft leads the way whilst the second weaves to left and right to cover our tail. Not only do we have the problem of the exercise tactical scenario, but also there are real dangers. As we descend we slow down and begin to call out

An air trooper of 2 Flight Army Air Corps provides close protection for the Gazelle helicopters at a forward airfield

35

hazards as soon as they are seen: 'wires left to right 500 metres', 'birds two o'clock'. As if this were not enough we have to avoid livestock, standing crops and a myriad of other obstacles. All this with a notional enemy gunning for us. But the speed is slowing now, even though the pressure is still on. We edge up a small re-entrant to the top of a ridge, while the second aircraft creeps along a woodline 200 metres to the left. Our position is too exposed, so we have to back off and try again half a mile to our right. Success! Between the two aircraft we can now see all of our target area. As we are studying the area, a Land-Rover appears with an orange cross on the side; this is our enemy tank for the day. We note the direction of travel and radio the information back to base. Given the order to use the guns we go ahead and, using well-practised procedures, call down the full weight of fire from a notional battery of Abbott self-propelled guns.

Mission accomplished, we head for home, though it's not just a case of turn tail and run as fast as we can. We slide back from our observation positions and pick our way back to the rear area. After all, there is still the threat of enemy anti-aircraft missiles. To cause minimum inconvenience to the locals, the flight commander calls an end to the tactical phase of the exercise and we begin a climb from what is colloquially known as the 'weedosphere' up to the dizzy height of 1,000 feet. As we start to climb we accidentally cut across the bottom of the garden of a large, secluded house. The owner has seen us and is even more surprised than we are; after all, she was sunbathing nude by the side of the pool!

Back in the office and it's time for constructive criticism. Every aspect of the trip is analysed to see where we went wrong and how we can prevent it happening next time. If we flew a perfect mission every trip then there would be no need to train, but then in a perfect world we would not need an Army and I would be out of a job. At the end of the debriefing we are all still on speaking terms and no one disagrees violently with the criticism of his performance, which is what you would expect from anyone who aspires to take their profession seriously.

The sortie has taken something over four hours to complete, for a little over an hour and a half in the air. A late lunch consists of a NAAFI pie and a cup of tea while everyone attempts to sort out their 'personal admin', the Army's great catch-all phrase for anything from writing letters to darning socks.

While we have been away the two Scouts have returned from providing DZ cover and are parked outside the hangar. A third has just returned from an overnight trip to Otterburn in the north-east of England where it has been helping to move personnel and matériel around the ranges. This leaves just two aircraft out working: the Gazelle which went out this morning, and a Scout which is out practising abseiling drills on the far side of the airfield. Half an hour later the Gazelle returns from task, followed shortly afterwards by the Scout.

The ground crew can now work to refuel, clean the squashed bugs off the bubble and put the aircraft to bed. The ground crews within the Army Air Corps are generally the unsung heroes behind everything we do. Everyone sees the helicopters and wants to ask about them. However, without the unseen help of ground crew, from the soldier who refuels the aircraft to all the

Lynx helicopters in action

technicians who keep those aircraft serviceable, there would be no flying at all.

The 30th of June ends with making last-minute arrangements for the annual Squadron Open Day. By 1800 hours we are able to call it a day. The aircraft are safely hangared and the technicians have assured themselves that those cowboy pilots haven't damaged any of their babies.

Passing-Out Parade at the WRAC Centre

The Army could not function without the Women's Royal Army Corps. Indeed its strength is about to be doubled from about 5,000 to 10,000. Here we are taken through a day at the WRAC Headquarters in Guildford.

It's 0530 hours, and the sound of birdsong rings around Queen Elizabeth Park, Guildford, the home of the Women's Royal Army Corps. At the gatehouse the milk float arrives with the daily delivery and Tim Tyler, the milkman who has served the Centre for many years, starts his rounds. The regimental police and duty staff also commence their morning rounds; opening up buildings, checking security and turning off the security lights. The cooks on the 'early shift' enter the Elizabethan Restaurant and start preparing breakfast for some 400 hungry servicewomen.

Meanwhile, in two of the Training Company accommodation blocks there is an air of excitement, for today there is a passing-out parade. It is the finale of two of the recruit courses: the Regular recruits have spent eight weeks at the WRAC Centre completing an intensive course which provides a young woman with all the basic military skills which she will require to be able to take her place alongside her male counterpart in the modern British Army. They have been an action-packed eight weeks, with map reading, first aid, nuclear, biological and chemical warfare instruction, weapon training, fieldcraft, physical training and a myriad of other subjects to prepare the recruit for her chosen career. The Territorial Army recruits have spent only fourteen days in Guildford, having travelled from their units scattered throughout the United Kingdom. They have left behind their civilian employment and all their other commitments to undertake their basic military training. Amongst their ranks are housewives and mothers with teenage children, civil servants, factory workers, teachers, secretaries, a roofer and a self-employed graphic design artist. They too have mastered the fundamentals of the Common Military Syllabus and will continue to build on the foundations laid at the WRAC Centre when they return to their units.

By 0700 hours the 120 recruits of the junior intake, who are in their fourth week of training, have finished cleaning their rooms and join the centipede of recruits marching in small groups towards the Elizabethan Restaurant. At home most were never up at this hour, and breakfast was either a meal only to be enjoyed at the weekend or eaten hastily prior to catching the bus to work. Now it is an essential part of the day and young recruits quickly learn that a good breakfast is vital if they are to survive another demanding day.

The platoon commander reports her platoon ready for inspection to the inspecting officer at a passing-out-parade at the WRAC Depot in Guildford

39

Outside the birdsong has been replaced by the sound of a military band marching up the road. Following close behind is the parade, 140 recruits and eighteen staff who are taking part in a rehearsal for today's parade with the band, which is the Pegasus Band of the Parachute Regiment. They are standing in for the WRAC Staff Band who are away on an important engagement in Eastbourne and who have only recently returned from a tour in BAOR. After two circuits of the massive parade ground, said to be one of the largest in Great Britain, everyone is satisfied and the recruits return to their accommodation while the band retires for some well-earned refreshments.

During all the activity on the square, 5 Platoon have been working away in the gym doing circuit training under the watchful eyes of the Physical Training Instructors. During their course each recruit will complete forty-four periods of PT and a further twenty periods of games and sports. In addition to the muscle-stretching circuits, the recruits tackle endurance runs of up to six and a half miles, aerobics, assault courses and the Military Swimming Test. They will certainly leave the Centre much fitter than when they arrived, but not without a few bumps and bruises sustained along the way.

'Left, left, left, right, left' – the familiar sound drifts across Queen Elizabeth Park as 6 Platoon march to the armoury to return the sub-machine-guns after two periods of weapon training. WRAC recruits have been doing weapon training only since July 1988, but they quickly master the skills of stripping and assembling, cleaning and preparing, before they progress to live firing on the ranges. The WRAC recruits have proved to be excellent shots and many of the scores achieved would be the envy of their male counterparts. One of the WRAC Weapons Instructors looks on as the weapons are handed in at the armoury.

A peaceful calm settles across the Centre for a short time before the parade. However, it does not extend to the Regimental Headquarters, where the Adjutant appears to be becoming somewhat heated on the telephone as a local unit announce that a helicopter will be arriving at 1130 hours to collect maps from the adjoining map depot. Eventually she convinces the caller that the timing is somewhat inconvenient as the square will be fully occupied by the parade; a revised time is agreed and another crisis is averted. Just time for a cup of coffee, she thinks, but she will have to make it herself as the office is short staffed, with the Corporal Clerk away representing the Corps at the celebrations to mark the tenth anniversary of the Queen Mother being appointed Lord Warden of the Cinque Ports. The Adjutant abandons the idea of a coffee and hurries towards the Officers' Mess where the Inspecting Officer is due to arrive shortly. Her progress is delayed by the 400 parents and friends who have all decided to move to the edge of the parade ground to ensure they get good seats for the parade. The aroma of lunch wafts from the Elizabethan. Today they serve over 700, as most of the visitors will join the recruits for the meal.

At 1100 hours all is set and the parade ground is filled by the long ranks of the 180 members of Training Company and the Pegasus Band all awaiting the arrival of the Inspecting Officer, Brigadier Mike Scott DSO CBE, who commanded the 1st Battalion of the Scots Guards in the Falklands War. The junior recruits sit on the edge of the parade ground to witness the parade and to learn

The inspecting officer reviewing the passing-out platoon

what they must achieve after a further four weeks' training. They are joined by forty members of the WRAC Association London Branches. It is a good few years since most of them were serving, and the memories will soon be flooding back. There are also nine members of the Kent Army Cadet Force, so one side of the parade ground represents three generations of servicewomen. The Parade Commander brings the parade to attention as the staff car draws up – the video cameras whir as fathers and brothers jockey for the positions with the best view. Everyone stands for the general salute – they may be civilian guests, but they have studied the programme avidly and have learnt what to do. The Inspecting Officer, accompanied by the Commandant and the Parade Commander, head for 1 Platoon who are the first to be inspected. There follows a slow procession as the Inspecting Officer progresses along the ranks of extremely proud recruits and Training Staff. While the band plays incidental music the recruits struggle not to sway to the tones of the well-known tunes.

Where do you come from? What trade are you going to follow? Have you enjoyed the course? Why did you join the Army? What have you learnt about yourself during training? These are amongst the questions the Inspecting Officer asks the recruits. To one side of the square the stretcher party from Headquarters and Holding Company hover ready to remove any casualties to the medical centre. They won't be needed today, as the Inspecting Officer is just finishing his inspection of the band, and the parade will shortly be on the move. The bass drum beats and the parade sets off as one to march twice past the Inspecting Officer. The platoon commanders shout their commands and the recruits manoeuvre into the required formations. Past the saluting dais in perfectly straight lines, shoes glinting in the sun and heads held high. The TA bring up the rear, dressed in their lightweight trousers, boots and shirts; many a member of staff and Regular recruit wishes that they were dressed the same, as the sun is high in the sky and their No 2 dress is somewhat warm. Minutes later the band strikes up again and leads the parade off the square. No longer recruits, but trained servicewomen; amongst the smiles there is the occasional tear, as it is almost the end of recruit training.

As the platoons march towards the assembly hall for a short church service and the Inspecting Officer's address and presentation of awards, a minibus pulls away from the selection centre. Inside are five potential recruits who have just spent twenty-four hours being briefed, tested, interviewed and assessed. Having spent a night in accommodation which is the same as the recruits' and having had the opportunity to talk to some of the recruits in the Sandes Coffee Shop last night, they have an excellent idea about their future career. All five have been offered the vacancies they wanted: one to be a military policewoman, another a driver, the third to train as an administrative assistant, while the other two are destined to be a staff clerk and a telecommunications operator. They have been guaranteed vacancies and will all return to the Centre next month to start their recruit training. In the meantime there is much to be achieved before they too will march off the parade ground as trained servicewomen.

At last the formal part of the proceedings is over and the recruits are united with their friends and relations. As the recruits recount all sorts of 'anglers' tales' about the last eight weeks of training, the Inspecting Officer and Commandant mingle with the visitors, who have travelled from all corners of the United Kingdom and a few from further afield. After half an hour the gathering breaks up and the recruits escort their visitors off to lunch, or on a tour of camp for yet more photographs. Brigadier Scott is taken to the Sergeants' Mess to meet the Mess members, all of whom have played vital parts either as instructors or in the administrative support of the recruits' training, prior to lunching in the Officers' Mess.

Before going for their lunch the Physical Training Instructors must complete the last of their duties as ushers. In addition to controlling the visitors during the parade, they have been collecting for the WRAC Association and the collection boxes must be returned to Corps Headquarters. As the corporals head for lunch they pass a recruit from the TA platoon shepherding her visitors toward the museum, where she is convinced that she has found a photograph of her mother, who served in the Auxiliary Territorial Service in 1944.

While the recruits and their visitors enjoy the day, the staff and students of the Warrant Officers' and Non-Commissioned Officers' Wing continue their work. Twenty-four potential corporals are approaching the climax of their Corporals' course, and this afternoon they will be tackling the practical command tasks which are designed to test their leadership skills and their ability to solve practical problems. The students on the nine-and-a-half-day course represent twelve different WRAC trades: range assistants, analysts, military accountants, cooks, kennelmaid, medical assistant, switchboard operator, stewardess, supply specialist, movement controller, telecommunications technician and postal and courier operator. Tomorrow they will go back to their units, which are scattered from Hong Kong to Berlin, Northern Ireland and all over Great Britain.

The junior recruits have all gone to Aldershot to take their Military Swimming Test and to have chest X-rays. The senior recruits have gone out with their visitors, before they return to pack ready for their departure to their trade training in the morning. The students on the Corporals' course have solved most of the command tasks and have returned to their syndicate rooms to be debriefed. The Adjutant is back at her desk as a helicopter lands on the square. It is not the one to collect maps, but a VIP helicopter bearing the Minister to the Armed Forces. The Adjutant hastens out to see him to his car, which is waiting on the edge of the square. The WRAC Centre helicopter landing site is often used by visiting dignitaries, and as he leaves the Minister tells the Adjutant that he wishes to visit the unit in the autumn. A group of potential servicewomen watch the activity as they complete their one-mile run as part of the selection procedure. In the Elizabethan Restaurant the shift has changed and tea is being prepared; the duty staff will be in for an early meal shortly.

The civilian staff put out the empty milk bottles and leave the camp, another day's work done, and the regimental police staff in the guardroom check to see that all the recruits have booked in and that all the visitors have been booked out. The junior recruits set about their evening tasks while the seniors pack and then head for the NAAFI for their end-of-course party. Elsewhere, in the Warrant Officers' and Non-Commissioned Officers' Wing accommodation, there is another end-of-course party in full swing. The Orderly Officer inspects the duty staff on staff parade and then goes on her rounds to check the perimeter fence. The regimental police secure the buildings, and as dusk falls the Orderly Officer is on her rounds again to check the NAAFI.

By 2300 hours all is quiet as the majority of the unit prepares for bed. Just as birdsong awoke the unit, an owl is heard calling as it flies its nightly patrol over Queen Elizabeth Park. Another day at the WRAC Centre draws to a close.

The Maritime Arm: 17 Port Regiment, Royal Corps of Transport

The Royal Corps of Transport is responsible, for the most part, for the provision of land transport to support the Army's logistics needs. Here we see a less well known side of the Corps' life – its maritime arm.

At first, all he could see was the glint of water and the dark outline of the Isle of Wight, across the Solent. Gradually, almost imperceptibly, the light strengthened and soon he could make out the shape of boats, the mexeflote causeway and the patchwork of woods and fields on the island. Standing silently in his trench, dug into the shingle on Browndown Beach, Driver Oliver looked along the sights of his light machine gun. If the enemy was going to attack, this was always the most likely and dangerous time.

52 Composite Port Squadron, one of the two regular operational squadrons in 17 Port Regiment RCT, was on exercise. Nearby, the remainder of the squadron was stirring after a brief respite in a busy twenty-four period. Some would have had no sleep. Ramped Craft Logistic and mexeflote rafts had been arriving regularly throughout the night, continuing the build-up of vehicles and ammunition which had been going on for the past two days. It looked as though it was going to be another fine day. If the weather held and there was no attack, the build-up should soon be complete.

As a Class 2 Port Operator, Driver Oliver had already played a full part in the discharge of many of the vessels, but everyone took their turn at sentry duty in the trenches protecting the squadron location. And now, as dawn broke, Driver Oliver kept a watchful eye on the slowly lightening coastline. The horizon cleared, and the dark outline of an anchored vessel developed into the clear grey shape of one of 51 Port Squadron's Ramped Craft Logistic (RCL), which had been attached to 52 Port Squadron for the duration of the exercise. In the wheelhouse of RCTV *Audemer*, Corporal Fisher rubbed his tired eyes and looked along the thirty-three-metre length of the RCL and its now empty cargo deck, capable of carrying up to ninety-six tonnes of vehicles or freight. The crew had been busy running cargo and vehicles on a waterborne Main Supply Route until just after midnight. As a Class 2 Navigator, Corporal Fisher was mate of the RCL, and was often called upon to command and navigate the vessel through coastal waters as far afield as Norway and Portugal. The RCL's crew of six men, all RCT seamen and marine engineers, allowed a two-watch system to operate. The 'skipper', or coxswain, ran one and the mate the other.

In the command post further back from the beach, Corporal Williams, the duty radio operator, was decoding a message which had just been received. 'RFA *Sir Percivale* now due your location 0900 hrs. Two hundred passengers and one hundred vehicles plus containers and freight for discharge.' He passed the message to the duty watchkeeper. Lieutenant Male read it and smiled to himself. He was looking forward to this. It would be very different unloading the ship across the beach to the routine operation in Marchwood Military Port. Everything would have to be unloaded at anchorage on to mexeflote rafts and then brought ashore. Vehicles would then drive off, up the roller trackway which had been laid like a silver ribbon across the soft shingle of the beach, and formed up in marshalling areas before moving on to their destination. Containers and freight, craned down on to the raft from the deck of the LSL, would be lifted off by the giant Fiat Allis fork-lift trucks. He looked at his watch – 0445 hours, just over an hour to go before breakfast.

Back at the Military Port in Marchwood, the working day for the remainder of the regiment would not start for another hour and a half. Apart that is from those on duty. Security is a high priority in all military establishments, and sentries are constantly on patrol, twenty-four hours a day.

At 0630 hours the first of the early risers entered the cookhouse for breakfast. Army food might once have been something of a joke, but certainly not any more. The standards are as good as any first class hotel. Fresh grapefruit, bacon and eggs and piping hot coffee and rolls. A good solid start to the day.

In the Sergeants' Mess, Sergeant Allen finished his breakfast and walked across to the armoury. A group of soldiers were already there, collecting their rifles ready to go to the rifle range. He called the roll. Two men still missing, but plenty of time yet. Sergeant Allen always liked to be ready early, to have everything buttoned up before the Troop Commander arrived: it got things off to a good start. He ran through his check list: ammunition, radios, first aid, packed meals. . . Everything in order and the last two men just arriving now. Perfect. 'Good morning, sir, last man just collecting his weapon – ammunition and stores all loaded in the truck – ready to go in two minutes.' It would be a good day. Just twenty-five men on the range. Today they would have their annual personal weapon test. Those waiting to fire would receive first aid instruction, and then afterwards everyone would spend some time in the gas chamber wearing NBC kit. Constant training and familiarisation give everyone more confidence in their equipment and their ability to survive a chemical attack in war.

By now the camp was coming to life properly. Those not on exercise, shooting on the range or included in particular duties, were gathering outside the gymnasium. The PTI appeared carrying two footballs and everyone relaxed slightly. He was a good PTI, he made PT fun and didn't just stick to PT and running – but there was no messing about either and he doubled them across the barracks to the football pitch, where in the next half hour they worked as hard playing football as they would have done in the gymnasium.

Meanwhile, as the Quay Foreman (the Warrant Officer in charge of Port Operations), WO2 Barker, walked down the Port South road, five vehicles loaded with ammunition rumbled past him. The duty plant operator, Lance-Corporal Adcock, was just finishing the first parade service on his equipment – a Henley Hermes fork-lift truck with a twenty-five-ton lifting capacity. He had hoped there would be time for a quick cup of tea but it wasn't to be. The first container wagon was already waiting outside with two containers for Kenya. Just as he finished dealing with that, another two containers arrived. . . .

Up until eleven o'clock everything went pretty well, when just as you start thinking to yourself that's the last one for a while, lo and behold another wagon turns up. It was quite pleasant to get a radio call at 1115 hours to say 'stop doing the container wagons, we're starting the *Arakan*.' This job consisted of picking up thirty-six containers from the jetty where they were being unloaded from HMAV *Arakan* (one of the two Army Landing Craft Logistic) and moving them to the container park. Quite a job to keep up with the crane. You tend to get one behind, then suddenly, before you know it, the number on the jetty seems to have multiplied. Well, it was just into lunchtime and word came to stop – but almost immediately that was changed, and we were working through to get the ship finished. Working part of lunchtime had a slight advantage for me because it meant I now had a bit more time to load the container rail set. Twenty containers later, the movements NCO came out with the rest of my day's details – five trailers to cross-load ready for the Bicester lads to pick up later in the afternoon. As it was getting late, it was time to recruit the assistance of a second machine to get the job done on time. . . .

Browndown Beach 0900 hours almost to the minute, and RFA *Sir Percivale* is dropping anchor 400 yards offshore. An RIB (Rigid Inflatable Boat with a ninety-horsepower outboard engine, capable of nearly forty knots) races out to meet her with the operations captain and a customs officer on board. Customs clearance is a necessary peacetime requirement, but it doesn't interfere too seriously with the exercise. On the beach, the 'Beachmaster' (the staff sergeant in charge of beach operations), Staff Sergeant McRobb, is getting impatient. The wind is beginning to get up and he is keen to be started. The stern ramp is down almost as quickly as the anchor and the first mexeflote raft is soon manoeuvring into position. . . .

It's nearly 1000 hours before the first mexeflote raft brings ashore an assortment of Land-Rovers, trailers and four-tonners. Again, inexperienced drivers – if I have to say 'low ratio, low gear' once more I think I'll thump someone! The discharge goes smoothly. By 1330 hrs it is complete and I've managed to throw some lunch down and grab another brew. The next job is to reconfigure the mexeflote rafts so that they can be used for other tasks. This is hazardous at the best of times, using a crane and the natural motion of the sea to lock and unlock the mexeflote cells. It's not easy when the wind is force two or three – but by now it is blowing force six with a sea state to match and it is becoming dangerous. As the wind continues to rise it is decided to postpone the operation until it moderates – too many men's fingers and hands at stake! The flotes are secured to the beach by their bow lines, using one of the 'Fiats' with a bucket like a bulldozer, to bury the lines and hold them fast.

Staff Sergeant McRobb supervising the loading of vehicles on to a Royal Corps of Transport craft at the military Port of Marchwood near Southampton

1800 hrs – more food, another brew and this time enough for seconds. I can be more leisurely now – my next real deadline is 2000 hours when the OC's 'O Group' is held. I contemplate a quick thirty minutes in my sleeping bag, but by the time I've checked on the sentries again it's too late.

After the 'O Group' I'm in the picture for the tasking over the next twenty-four hours. My priority is to get the mexeflote reconfiguration completed. The wind has moderated by 2100 hrs so we start where we left off, completing the job by 0200 hrs the next morning. Check the sentries one more time then I'm in my sleeping bag by 0230 hrs – luxury – a lie-in now until 0530 hrs! . . .

Back in Marchwood the 'routine' operation of the port had continued. With half the regiment away on exercise and some on the range, the remainder had been busy. WO2 Barker, the Quay Foreman, hadn't stopped:

Started to load the first mexeflote raft with ammunition for MV *Puma* (a chartered merchant ship carrying ammunition to the continent for troops in Germany), at 0950 hours. By 1130 hours the load was complete and slipped, bound for Netley Buoys where the *Puma* is anchored. I can now split the 'shore side' gang and start to load the RCL with the remaining ammunition and the two twenty-foot containers. It is 1230 hours. I book the late meals at 1430 hours for everyone, and organise the loading of fifty pallets for the exercise – working through lunch to get the vessel away as quickly as possible. Break for lunch – half an hour and then back again. By now phone calls into and out of my office average one every thirty seconds. I dream of somewhere quiet where no one can find me. By 1600 hours the load on RFA *Sir Geraint*, which has been going on all afternoon, is complete to the Chief Officer's satisfaction. The RCL is back. Everyone is clearing up. 1650 hours – I take a final walk round. Everything away. I close down the port operations office. Suddenly the port looks deserted. I walk back up to the top gate. Another day over. . . .

The Army Catering Corps

Major M W Herriott ACC

Napoleon is supposed to have said, 'An army marches on its stomach.' Here we see a typical day in the life of the Army Catering Corps.

No 4 Region Army Catering Service (UK) has its headquarters in York. Responsible to the General Officer Commanding the Military District, their task is to ensure the required catering services are provided daily for some 12,000 Regular and 11,000 Territorial Army soldiers throughout the north-east of England. Each unit has a team of ACC chefs allocated to it, led by a Master Chef. Every infantry battalion has some twenty chefs led by a Warrant Officer, whilst a smaller training unit might have only eleven chefs, led by a Staff Sergeant. In civilian parlance Major Mike Herriott, who runs No 4 Region, could be described as the 'District Catering Operations Manager', and as such he arranges for each of the twenty Master Chefs to receive regular visits from one of the team of three Area Catering Officers (ACOs) or six Area Catering Warrant Officers (ACWOs). Progress is monitored and difficulties reported.

Lieutenant-Colonel Gordon Wilkinson has responsibility for two military districts and looks after 'England north of the Wash'. His office and that of Major Herriott are side by side in York. On 30 June Colonel Wilkinson was at his desk catching up on policy matters after having been away for several days visiting units in the Liverpool area and attending an Army Catering Corps Promotion Selection Board held at Exeter. He actually wears out suitcases in this job. That day was, for the Colonel, devoted to a succession of telephone calls and a stack of files, most with 'urgent' tags pinned on them. It was Major Herriott's turn to get out of the office, having held the fort whilst his leader had been away. Accompanied by Warrant Officer Bill Morgan, ACWO for the York area, he spent the day visiting 16 Air Defence Regiment, Royal Artillery, near Scunthorpe in Lincolnshire.

Meanwhile, further north at Catterick Garrison near Darlington, Captain Brian Hymers, one of the two ACOs in that garrison, was involved in managing the provision of lunch for His Majesty King Olav of Norway. The King, in his capacity as Colonel-in-Chief of 1st Battalion The Green Howards (Alexandra, Princess of Wales's Own Yorkshire Regiment), was paying a visit to present new Colours upon the occasion of the regiment's tercentenary celebrations. Captain Hymers had selected Sergeant Christopher Evans, serving with 8 Signal Regiment, also at Catterick, to prepare lunch for the King.

Sergeant Chris Evans at work in a typical Army kitchen

Chris Evans is something of a star and was a finalist in the 'Army Chef of the Year' competition in 1989. He made it all seem easy, producing an excellent meal, and the lunch party at the Commanding Officer's residence went off without a hitch.

Captain Hymers didn't stay to see the coffee served because he then went on to visit another of his garrison units, namely the Duchess of Kent's Military Hospital. Joined by the Master Chef, Warrant Officer Bill McSeveny, he toured the hospital wards to talk to the patients and staff to ensure that his customers were content and that all their respective dietary requirements were being met. It is not always easy to keep Warrant Officer McSeveny's mind on catering, because he is a rugby referee of note and when not on parade with his whistle he is usually talking or planning rugby. However, in June, rugby is still some time away and his formidable catering expertise was well in evidence in the hospital.

Captain Brian Hymers and WO2 Bill McSeveny chat to Mr Sam Samgate, a patient of theirs, in the Duchess of Kent Military Hospital

Elsewhere in Catterick that day, another member of the team, Warrant

Officer Dunston was busy ensuring that the enormous catering support required by the 1st Battalion The Green Howards for their tercentenary celebrations was running smoothly. In view of the size of the commitment, an outside catering contractor had to be called in to help provide lunch for 1,400 people in a large marquee on the garrison sports ground. Quite correctly, the ACS insists that such contractors produce the same standards of catering that are expected of the ACC. It fell to Warrant Officer Dunston to ensure the service was up to an impeccable standard, not an easy task in the boiling heat of the summer of 1989. In this business, as soon as one meal is complete there is a need to start on the next, and the ACC chefs of the battalion, lunch behind them, had now to prepare for the functions to be held that evening in the Officers', and Warrant Officers' and Sergeants' Messes for 180 and 350 people respectively. No fuss, no bother, but hard physical work nevertheless, with high job satisfaction when it's all over.

All in all, a not untypical day in Catterick, which houses one of the largest garrisons in the Army, composed of a diverse range of units and all catered for by No 4 Region. Happily there were no reports of scurvy, beri beri or other ailments caused by malnutrition!

The Territorial Army now constitutes a vital element of the British Army and has to be supported in the same way as the Regular Army. One of No 4 Region's officers, Captain James Knowles, supported by Warrant Officer Ronald Fowles, spends much of his time advising, instructing and inspecting the catering operations of TA units the length and breadth of northern England. On 30 June 1989, Captain Knowles and Warrant Officer Fowles were visiting the Army's transit training camp at Scarborough to ensure that 35 Signal Regiment (V) from London on their annual summer training camp were enjoying a satisfactory standard of catering. This is particularly important when one considers that the TA soldier is fed by a TA chef, and although that TA chef wears an ACC cap badge, he can be recruited from any walk of life ranging from bus driver to company director, to sewerage worker. They are a wonderful bunch of men who seem to find the hard physical work involved therapeutic. They really are a special breed.

The ACC are busy . . . always. Caterers live in the real world, not for them exercise followed by exercise, because they do for real in peace what they would do in war and they wouldn't want to change that. Feeding soldiers is not a glamorous business; for the most part it is an administrative function that goes unnoticed. However, feeding is critical and soldiers who are unfed can't fight, indeed after about forty-eight hours they fall over! That didn't happen on 30 June 1989 and it won't happen at any time in the future if the Army Catering Corps has anything to do with it!

Serving to Lead at RMA Sandhurst

The Royal Military Academy Sandhurst is famous throughout the world. In this chapter we are able to witness a typical day in its life.

The thirtieth of June 1989 begins early for some of the officer cadets of the Royal Military Academy Sandhurst. It is just past midnight and many of the cadets from Old College are guarding well-concealed patrol bases in remote valleys and woods up in the Welsh hills near Sennybridge. They have been on exercise for a week, learning and practising the techniques of counter-revolutionary warfare in a rural setting. This particular setting is very authentic and the cadets have had only the company of sheep during their enthusiastic quest for insurgents. The weather is not kind, having rained steadily for most of the week, fully endorsing everyone's suspicions that the Sennybridge hills conjure up their own unique climate.

Most of these seemingly alert young men, acting as sentries for their sleeping comrades, are soaked to the skin and looking forward to a little sleep themselves before the final push against the enemy. The sentries begin waking up the patrol base. 'Half an hour to be ready in all respects for the move', the orders said. Two hours for the approach march to the enemy's encampment and everyone to be in position before the first hints of dawn.

Sleep-drugged figures stumble quietly around their bivouacs, feeling for the last few items of rain-sodden kit to stow in their bergens. The Directing Staff are out and about, unobtrusively encouraging, cajoling and even hissing the occasional order until the column moves off.

The enemy's base, a disused farmhouse, has been examined in great detail by an earlier reconnaissance patrol and everyone knows, in theory at least, how to reach it and what to do on arrival. The drills begin to take over . . . movement by night, how to react to any unexpected encounters en route . . . and a myriad of other details, talked about in the classroom, practised back in the Academy grounds and now for 'real'. The march is reasonably uneventful, insofar as this is possible moving ninety fully-equipped men through a dense, damp forest in the dark, but the Company arrives at its final rendezvous intact and on time. The next trick is to divide the Company into 'cut-off' groups and an assault group, for the delicate business of closing with and capturing or destroying the enemy. The leaders of the groups take command and move silently towards their predesignated positions on the approaches to the farm. The area around the farm had been described in detail the evening before, during the orders for the attack. Now the importance of certain landmarks and reference points becomes clear; each group knows what to do for the attack.

53

The most frustrating aspect of this preparatory phase is the waiting period before the attack is triggered. Every man has moved into position and must remain silent and unobserved until the critical moment. The rain continues, as does the struggle to stay warm and awake.

The brain drifts back to full consciousness now that there is a vague hint of light spreading across the eastern sky. At last, at about 0345 hours, the farm buildings become defined against the woods and fields beyond. Soon the enemy – Gurkhas from Sandhurst's own demonstration company – can be observed moving about their base.

A long burst of fire from a machine-gun shatters the dawn and, before the echoes die away down the valleys, the attack is under way. There is theatrical panic in the enemy base as they react to the noise and weight of firepower. Few well-laid plans survive after the initial exchange of fire, and our famous Gurkha insurgents are not going to give up without one of their renowned fights. They swiftly organise a counter-attack and fight their way out of the farm buildings, heading off in a most unexpected direction, not at all within the design of battle envisaged by the officer cadet commanding the operation. He gives fresh orders to his nearest cut-off group to redeploy rapidly. The resulting action is a combined display of enthusiastic pursuit by the cadets and good-natured acceptance of inevitable defeat by the insurgents. The farm and its outbuildings are captured, together with several prisoners. Those that have tried to escape have been either 'killed' or rounded up. All in all, a good conclusion to a well planned and executed attack, and a good note upon which to end the exercise. A thoroughly satisfying breakfast follows the post-mortem of the exercise, and it is still only 0530 hours!

The coach trip back to the Academy is remembered by few, as the dirty and damp officer cadets catch up on much lost sleep.

As the coaches slip quietly through the tolls on the Severn Bridge, the Royal Military Academy itself is beginning to come to life. One company starts the

You learn to sleep anywhere in the Army!

day with a military history lecture on the Second World War, another is being taught the skills of interviewing, both by the Academy's own academic staff. For the senior intakes and the Women's Standard Course, breakfast is followed by Military Technology. The lecture team comes from the Royal Military College of Science, where Army undergraduates read science degrees. They will give presentations on those aspects of engineering and science that are having an impact on the development of military equipment and systems. After the lecture the cadets are divided into groups of about twenty-five to discuss the implications of all that they have heard. The pattern will repeat itself throughout much of the day, with discussion following each presentation.

In Academy Headquarters another type of presentation is under way: 'All male and female officers are now trained at Sandhurst, the majority following either a forty-four-week course for male non-graduates, or a twenty-eight-week course for graduates and women officer cadets.' This time it is the home team briefing a visiting General about the Sandhurst courses. The length and content of the course has changed many times since the last war, and several high-ranking officers are updated each year. 'The training year follows much the same pattern as the conventional academic year, with the main intakes arriving at the beginning of the spring, summer and autumn terms and passing out after the respective twenty-eight- or forty-four-week courses. There is a great emphasis on sport and outdoor pursuits, and during the holidays the cadets are obliged to take part in adventurous training activities both in the UK and abroad.' The briefing continues, giving the General a complete picture of Sandhurst in 1989. Much has changed since he was at the Academy in 1959 and he will soon see just how much when he makes a personal tour of the Academy.

He begins, where present-day Sandhurst began, in Old Building. Courses have been run continually since 1812 in this part of the Academy, and with its impressive frontage, parade square and greensward leading down to the lake, it dominates the grounds. Behind the façade there are hundreds of rooms; most famous perhaps is the Indian Army Memorial Room directly behind the Grand Entrance, which doubles as a museum and an ornate function room. The rest of the rooms are in day-to-day use as ante-rooms, offices, accommodation, or halls or study. It is in one such hall of study that he encounters the TA Commissioning course, which is examining the art of patrolling. They are currently locked in animated detailed discussion with their platoon commander, an experienced infantry captain. Having established the finer points, the course moves out to the Barossa training area of gorse, bracken and small pine woods adjacent to the Academy. They act out roles and techniques under the watchful eye of their instructors. A position of all-round defence is adopted, prior to moving on towards an imaginary objective. It is hard to take it all seriously when practising during daylight, but as our friends in Wales found, controlling a mobile body of men at night, without getting lost and remaining undetected, is not easy. The visiting General smiles to himself as he watches the patrol reacting to an imaginary enemy ambush. This aspect of training has not changed at all. Cadets are in disarray, Directing Staff shouting advice and encouragement, and the imaginary enemy winning!

Three miles outside the Academy gates, the sleepers from Sennybridge are woken up, propped up and generally made to look like smart, alert soldiers entering a military environment. The homecoming procedure, even after a long and exhausting exercise, is well known. All weapons are cleaned and examined before being locked back into the armoury, then personal kit can be dealt with. Washing machines and dryers are kept busy for the rest of the day and much of the night.

The TA course's patrolling is coming on well and the visitor has moved on to see what the junior intake is doing. These officer cadets have been at the Academy since early May and are now well into their fourteen-week first term. Like the other intakes they are a mixture of schoolboy entrants, overseas cadets and ex-soldiers with varying degrees of experience and proficiency in the ranks. So far today they have been studying how orders for an operation are given and the particular way in which the Army goes about explaining a complex under-taking. When giving orders, much of the impact of what is said is derived from the stage management of the whole procedure. The General looks on as a cadet is singled out to deliver his orders to others from his platoon. He and his fellow cadets will have plenty of opportunity in the next two terms to practise this particular communication skill, and it is used extensively as a means of assessing cadets. Sandhurst's motto is 'Serve to Lead', and putting a cadet under pressure is just one way of developing leadership qualities.

With the details of ohms, amps, radiation dosages, and the speed of a new high-velocity missile fresh in their minds, the military technologists have exhausted their discussions and now find themselves on parade. After hearing about the latest methods of transporting troops about the battlefield, it is reas-suring to know that the leg, foot and boot still work! The General is impressed. He is taken back again to 1959, to the Sandhurst he remembers. Drill, he had been told thirty years ago, is a curious aspect of training. It epitomises many of the characteristics of good soldiering: attention to detail, speed of response to orders, and a sense of pride, and it forges a link with the traditions of the past. The pageantry of the Sovereign's Parade, when the senior cadets are formally commissioned and the Adjutant rides up the steps of Old Building on his white charger, goes back many years. So too does the humour in the Company Ser-geant Major's patter as he demands and gets higher and higher standards – 'Mr Smith, sir, at drill you are as much use as a window cleaner in Beirut.'

By late afternoon the clean-up following the Sennybridge exercise is nearly complete. For the Gurkhas who provided the enemy, however, there is still no rest. They are now in their full fighting order of dress, giving a very detailed and practical demonstration of patrolling to the TA course. This will clear up any mysteries from this morning's lesson and set the scene for tonight's exercise.

Overlapping with the men's TA course is a course for women TA officers. They have spent the morning in classrooms working through a command post exercise; they practise passing information and responding to the numerous and varied problems that would be posed in a real headquarters. Then, in con-trast to their sedentary morning, they have an orienteering competition in the afternoon, followed by a rehearsal for their Passing-Out Parade.

The visiting General departs from the Academy after tea. His short visit has given him much information about the courses but, more importantly, he now has an intimate feeling of how these young men and women, drawn from all walks of life, are trained. For him the high spot of the day was listening to the very earnest young man delivering an extremely good set of orders. The stage management was good, the model of the terrain excellent, but he attacked the wrong objective! He clearly remembers a similar young man under similar circumstances back in 1959!

By the time the General's car has nosed its way into London and home, most of the cadets are changing for dinner. Some, like the women's TA course, are dressing for their end-of-course party, while others are preparing to do battle during their night patrol exercise. The cadets on Academy guard duty are patrolling the grounds; those with enough money and energy are heading for the bright lights. All will have to be back for an 'at home' sports weekend against the Combined Naval Colleges of Manadon and Dartmouth. These keenly fought competitions make use of all the excellent sports facilities throughout the Academy: cricket, tennis and clay pigeon shooting in the grounds, golf, swimming in Sandhurst's own indoor pool, and even rowing on the lakes.

By midnight the end-of-course party is in full swing, but most cadets, like the General, are sound asleep. The guard continues its relentless search for suspicious people and packages. The patrol moves quietly from its position of all-round defence. It has successfully completed its task and is returning home. Another day in the life of Sandhurst.

Field Marshal Sir Nigel Bagnall inspecting officer cadets at the RMA Sandhurst during a Passing-Out Parade. Notice how the platoon he is inspecting has been 'sized' with the tallest men on the outside and the smallest in the middle. The cadets are carrying the SA-80 rifle

Preston Barracks, Brighton: The Territorial Army

The Territorial Army is an integral part of the Army. This chapter gives a fascinating insight into the 'other life' led by thousands of men and women throughout Britain. For the TA, 30 June has been stretched into the ensuing weekend, 1 and 2 July.

Preston Barracks was built before the Second World War for a cavalry regiment. It lies on the eastern outskirts of Brighton in East Sussex, and today is the home of three Territorial Army units, each representing a different part of the Army. The oldest is 583 (EOD) Squadron of the Royal Engineers, EOD standing for Explosive Ordnance Disposal. It was formed in 1981 and is now part of the new 101 (London) Engineer Regiment, the bomb disposal experts of the TA. Formed a year later is a detachment of 253 Provost Company, Royal Military Police (V), whose headquarters is at Tulse Hill in South London, with another detachment at Southampton. The newest unit, raised in 1986 as part of the TA's expansion programme, is B (Somme) Company of 6th/7th Battalion, The Queen's Regiment, an infantry unit.

In time of war, the men and women of the Territorial Army make up about one-third of the Army, providing more than half the infantry needed in BAOR and over sixty per cent of the Army's medical services. Without them this country could not meet its NATO and home defence commitments. The TA's members are all civilians during the day, busy at their own careers, and the training and experience volunteers get during their time in uniform provide a different perspective on life. Management and leadership training and experience for NCOs and officers, new skills training for everyone, and a very much higher level of fitness than that of the average civilian are benefits of their voluntary service.

In the fifty years since the TA was last called up for war there have been many changes. In 1939 the TA was poorly equipped. Today it is identically equipped to the Regular Army and is highly trained in at least one speciality.

This weekend is typical of many throughout the year. It started early for some with a trip to just north of the Scottish border to practise demolition techniques. Dalbeattie in Dumfries and Galloway is the site of a Second World War factory, the ugly remains of this building needing to be removed by the Scottish Development Agency. Two members of the permanent staff and four TA sappers under the command of the Permanent Staff Administration Officer, Captain Brian Batty, left by road early on Thursday morning. They had much to do, including drawing explosives and equipment from local depots, and liaison with the police and local authorities.

58

Friday evening back at Preston Barracks saw an increase in activity. At 1930 hours another forty volunteer sappers assembled in the TA Centre, and after drawing kit, boarded an Army coach for their long trip north. The senior TA officer is Lieutenant John Forbes.

At about the same time an advance party from the RMP detachment of ten volunteer 'redcaps' leave for a short journey to Thorney Island, where their company has planned a military skills training weekend. A number of activities have to be organised by the following morning so that the TA NCOs from all three detachments can be trained and tested in a variety of skills, from working on a range and map reading to first aid and driving.

Saturday morning at Brighton starts off with a flurry of activity. At 0600 some eighty volunteers from the Infantry Company are assembled under the charge of the company OC, Major Ron Dalby, a TA officer. They draw weapons and kit, check it, then into the transport for the journey to Hankley Common, an Army training area near Aldershot. At 0915 they arrive to spend the rest of the day practising such infantry techniques as ambushing, section and platoon attacks

The Territorial Army holds regular exchanges with overseas forces; pictured here, a TA infantry soldier on exercise with a United States National Guardsman

and patrolling. All this is very necessary preparation for the major exercises planned for later in the year when they will join with other battalions, Regular and TA, to practise their wartime role.

While all this is going on, far away to the north the volunteers of the Royal Engineers have arrived and are getting straight down to work. They work solidly until 1700 hours, drilling some 480 boreholes, each fourteen or fifteen inches deep, in the walls of the old torpedo factory which is scheduled for demolition on Sunday morning. This completed, the holes are charged with explosive, then all are joined with a detonator cord ring main. For Corporal Gary Elmer, whose day job is as a builder, this is a big change: during the week he puts them up, and at weekends he knocks them down!

Meanwhile at Thorney Island, one of the groups is under the charge of Corporal Alison Miller, whose civilian job is as a secretary, but at weekends she becomes a Women's Royal Army Corps Provost NCO. Nicknamed 'Alpha', she has the distinction of being the first woman, Regular or TA, to gain the coveted Provost Marshal's Gold Whistle award for being top on her recruits' course. Today, everyone had motorcycle and driver training. Handling a long-wheel-base Land-Rover with its trailer over rough ground is an art that needs plenty of practice.

In Scotland, by 0830 on the Sunday the sappers had cleared up the site, breakfasted, packed up their tents and kit, loaded the vehicles and parked them safely away from the danger area. The liaison officer and local police were on the nearby road, ready to stop the traffic. The officer in charge went forward to check that all was well and with a Permanent Staff Instructor laid out the electrical initiation cable and applied the detonators to the ring main they had fitted up the previous afternoon.

Everyone had to be behind the firing point, and after a final check that no one was in the danger area, the authority to fire was given. At 0900 promptly the youngest and newest recruit had the privilege of pressing the button. This time, Sapper Andrew Wright, a nineteen-year-old trainee accountant from Brighton, had that privilege. A loud bang echoed through the valley. When the smoke and dust died down, the factory had ceased to exist.

The sappers who had been involved in the preparation work could then go forward to see the devastation caused by the explosives. By 0930 they were all in their coaches for the long journey back to Brighton, for that evening they all became civilians again and had to be ready for their ordinary jobs on Monday.

Two years before, two TA soldiers met at an Army open day. Today they are Mr and Mrs Barnard, but for this weekend they are both in the uniforms of lance-corporals, both members of the sapper squadron, but in different sections. Brian, a twenty-year-old draughtsman, had seen it all before, but it was the first time for Jane, his nineteen-year-old wife, whose daytime job is as a telephonist. Another young woman, who helped sort out the yards of explosive cord on the Saturday, is a young mother, and at the weekends is Private Margaret Smith. A full-time mother, a part-time Sainsbury's stacker, and a part-time member of the TA. How does she fit it all in? That is a question many Regulars ask about each of the 75,000 or so volunteers who make up today's TA.

Privates Joanne Hilton and Andrew Smith of 583 EOD Squadron RE prove that men and women work together in today's TA

For the RMP at Thorney Island, Sunday morning brings watermanship tests, swimming and PT and a return to barracks after lunch. Perhaps the least welcome part of the TA's weekend is having to wash the Land-Rovers and motor cycles, and clean and store the kit, for all this equipment must always be ready for instant use.

Almost at the same time as the redcaps get back, so do the infantry from the Queens. They pile out of the transport, some still with traces of camouflage cream on their faces and various grasses and leaves still woven into their uniforms to break up their silhouettes. Despite thirty-six hours in the field they look a cheerful bunch, all prepared to swap 'war stories' in the mess after a clean-up before going home.

Territorial Army sappers pictured during a night drill session

Pass-Off Day at the Light Division Depot

All soldiers have to be trained. This look at a day in the life of the Light Division Depot shows us how it's done.

It is early morning and dawn has crept over the land with the suddenness characteristic of summer. The sky is already a clear, broad blue but it is not yet warm enough to tempt the thin mist from the fields and hedges. Nothing stirs save a falcon high above the heath, silent in its daily vigil.

For four members of the guard, returning from a patrol of the barrack perimeter, morning has come earlier than for most. For the past two hours they have provided part of the vital screen against the possibility of terrorist activity. Although barely two months into their training, these young men are armed and equipped as for operations. They move with a purpose and an assurance which belies their relative inexperience, using the cover available, constantly alert and alive to anything unfamiliar on their patrol route.

Soldiers have a way of adapting to change. Most of the recruits at the depot view guard duties as an onerous but vital part of their daily lives. Many look upon them as an opportunity to put training into practice, or as a means of getting their first introduction to the tasks that will face them should they be posted to Northern Ireland. None fails to realise the importance of security measures and the part that each has to play in their implementation.

As the patrol, now unloaded and debriefed, relax over a mug of tea and a cigarette, the depot slowly comes back to life around them. The new day centres customarily on the cookhouse. Already lines of recruits are filing past the hotplates to collect the Catering Corps' famous blend of humour and culinary excellence. For the majority, today is just another training day, but for one group of men breakfast has never tasted so good. For the thirty or so recruits of Calais Platoon, part of the Adult Training Company, today is the day towards which they have worked for the past five months. Pass-Off Day: the end of training and the gateway to battalion life.

After a breakfast taken at a marginally more leisured pace than normal, those recruits due to parade that day return to the platoon lines to add finishing touches to the uniforms and equipment to be worn later in the morning. Spit and polish and the mindless regime of kit preparation have never been guiding principles in the Light Division; nonetheless, each recruit takes a pride in his appearance and is at pains to ensure that his turnout is of the highest standard. Whether it be for family, friends or just for the occasion, appearance on the parade is viewed as a token for all the other skills learnt during the nineteen weeks of basic training.

Damn! I should have tried harder at the long jump at school

A glance around the accommodation reveals much to indicate the changes that have evolved in the training of recruits for the Division and the Army as a whole. The soldiers are now housed in five-man rooms; duvets, music systems and the occasional television are in evidence. Gone is the harshness of the typical barrack block. Chores are kept to sensible levels of cleanliness and tidiness – no more the mindless round of polishing and 'dagging' for their own sake. Similar changes in attitude have been in evidence throughout the training of these recruits, so much so that the unenlightened diehard points indignantly to an apparent decline in discipline and general standard. Not so: the recruit of

I need to lose some weight!

today is generally better educated and more enquiring than his counterpart of previous decades. He therefore requires and merits more enlightened treatment than the correction preferred previously. He is normally an individual who prefers to be convinced rather than compelled, to be motivated rather than threatened. He is an individual who through constructive and progressive training can be encouraged to think increasingly for himself in order to carry out his role as an infantryman.

By the time uniforms are donned and inspections completed, the time for the parade itself is drawing near. Almost five hundred friends and relatives have made the trip to Winchester, to encourage and support the recruits due to graduate to the status of trained Light Division soldiers. The contribution made by these visitors to the atmosphere and overall success of the day is considerable – for many of them, it is their first taste of the life now fully adopted by their sons, brothers and boyfriends who are now on parade. They are impressed at the speed and efficiency with which the spectacle unfolds. The marching at 140 paces per minute (noticeably swifter than the more conventional pace), the bugle calls in lieu of words of command and the famous final 'double-past' are all hallmarks of the distinctive style of the Division.

The parade complete, all repair to the NAAFI for the traditional celebratory drink. It is now that the marked effect of training can most clearly be felt. The recruits themselves have taken on a new air of self-confidence. Although many look forward with uncertainty and some apprehension to joining a battalion, all display a supreme contentment and relief that the rigours of basic training have been mastered. It is in the admiring, almost disbelieving, words of parents and friends, however, that the real achievement of training can be noted.

Strikingly, even as the newly-qualified trained infantrymen relax outside the NAAFI with their visitors, the process of coaching other recruits to that goal goes on relentlessly around them. A junior platoon, still weeks from their own Pass-Off Parade, marches slowly past, the fatigue of a day's fieldcraft training mixing with a look of envy on their faces as they notice the celebration of those for whom training is now a memory. In the distance a squad limbers up for physical training; they wear training shoes rather than boots, indicating that for them training is in its earliest stages. All in all a total of seventeen strands of training can progress at any one time, ranging from Adult platoons to Junior Leaders and Territorial Army recruits.

As evening draws in, an apparent peace descends once more on the depot. Training has been completed for the week, and the platoon which paraded for its Pass-Off today has now left the barracks for ten days' leave prior to posting to various battalions in England, Ulster and around Europe. The falcon still wheels in silence high in the cooling air above the statue of Sir John Moore, the spotlights flick on around the camp perimeter and once again a security patrol prepares to leave the gate.

The Irish Guards

*For many, the Guardsman in his red tunic epitomises the British
Army. This chapter shows us what the Brigade of Guards is really like.*

They're changing guard at Buckingham Palace –
Christopher Robin went down with Alice.
Alice is marrying one of the guard.
'A soldier's life is terrible hard,'

                Says Alice.

A A Milne, *When We Were Very Young*

Trooping the Colour on Horse
Guards Parade each year in
front of Her Majesty the Queen
is one of the major events in
the Brigade of Guards' calendar

If Alice were marrying one of the Irish Guards on duty at Buckingham Palace today, she would probably comment, not that his life is 'terrible hard' (though of course training is tough), but that it is terribly varied. Variety and fun are the real hallmarks of serving in the 'Micks' these days. 30 June 1989 found most of the battalion not on guard in bearskins and tunics, but enjoying the last day of a fortnight's shooting on the ranges at Salisbury Plain, on ISAAC.

The Army is full of initials: ISAAC stands for Infantry Skill At Arms Camp. During the two weeks of glorious sunshine, we all did our annual weapons, first aid and fitness tests. All infantrymen have to achieve high scores on their own personal weapon (usually the SA 80 rifle) and another (the Light Support Weapon – a machine-gun variant of the SA 80) alternative. We also have to run three miles in full kit (forty-four pounds including rifle and helmet) in thirty-three minutes; and demonstrate that we can give first aid, among other tests. Our ISAAC ended on 30 June with a shooting competition. All 650 men in the battalion were divided into teams of five, which had to run 100 metres and then shoot down twelve metal plate targets, four teams against each other at a time.

Like most soldiers' days, 30 June started early. The cooks were up at 0500 hours, preparing the usual early breakfast for men condemned to hard work. Reveille for the remainder was at 0600, as the transit camp we had been living in for the fortnight had to be handed over to the next inhabitants spick and span. After washing, cleaning, packing and breakfast, the companies departed for the ranges in four-tonne trucks: like most of the infantry, we fight on our feet, but generally travel in vehicles.

We had a visitor for our last day on the ranges: the Army Commander, Lieutenant-General Sir David Ramsbotham, who had commanded us in 3rd Armoured Division during our last tour in Germany, in 1985. Before going to the shooting competition, he visited one of the rifle companies doing selection tests for promotion to Lance Corporal. Forty Guardsmen in the battalion attend the promotion course; 4 Company was selecting their best men to go on the course later in the year. Every man took his turn in commanding his section of six or seven in a task designed to test his planning, leadership and coolheadedness under pressure. A temperature in the eighties and the Army Commander looking on added to the stress: testing circumstances for the Guardsmen to earn their places on the promotion course.

Naturally the glorious weather was a talking point with the General: he might be forgiven for thinking the Micks were a bit blasé about the temperature and the change of scene from London ceremonial duties.

'Pretty hot, eh?'

'Oh, it's all right, sir, it's nothing after Belize, sir.' (The battalion got back from a six-month tour there in April – our second Caribbean posting in nine years.)

'And it's not as hot as the Troop either, sir.' (Our ISAAC started straight after 'the Troop' – the Queen's Birthday Parade, in which many of the battalion, including this company, had taken part. It gets mighty hot in £2,000 of scarlet, gold and bearskin, parading all morning in the sunshine.)

'And it'll be hotter in Cyprus.' (120 men of the 650 in the battalion went off to Cyprus in September for a month.)

General Ramsbotham with members of 2 Company, the Irish Guards

Company Sergeant Major Kirkland administers 'first aid' to Lance-Corporal Parkins!

The General moved on to Support Company. Each infantry battalion has five companies. Headquarter Company contains the administrative staff of the battalion: clerks, cooks, drivers, mechanics, tailors, storemen and so on. Then there are three rifle companies of three platoons, each armed with the new rifle and its light machine-gun variant, anti-tank rockets and grenades. Finally there is a support weapons company, which contains the mortar platoon (their eight 81mm mortars are the battalion's own artillery); the Milan platoon, with Milan anti-tank missiles; the signals platoon, which provides all our communications; and the reconnaissance platoon, which moves ahead of the rest of the battalion on operations, scouting out the lie of the land and the enemy. All these specialist platoons are manned by selected men who have already proved themselves in rifle platoons. Groups of new men drafted from the rifle companies were being introduced to their new weapons as the Army Commander went round. Some were getting their first experience of Wombat, the anti-tank gun which is issued along with Milan missiles to anti-tank platoons in Berlin battalions: the battalion moves to Berlin in 1990 for two-and-a-half years.

'Lovely weather – bit hot, eh?'

'Not as hot as it was on HMS *Boxer*.' (There is a constant flow of Micks visiting our affiliated Royal Navy ship, the destroyer HMS *Boxer*; some of Support Company had just joined her for a Channel cruise.)

'Oh, it's hot, sir, but it was worse at the athletics last week.' (The previous week the battalion athletics team had won the zonal championships, beating all the other teams from the London, South-Eastern and Eastern military districts: athletics, soccer and boxing are the main Irish Guards sports, but we also have three Army cricketers, one of the top three cycling teams, the Army racquets champions, good cross-country, squash and tennis teams; and our rugby team once beat the Welsh Guards.)

'Oh sir, it was hotter yesterday on the March and Shoot.' (Over the past two days, the platoons had all competed in a punishing forced march against the clock, followed by a shooting match.)

By 0930, when the General arrived, the shooting competition was in full swing. The teams waited in company ranks, to do what the British infantry has always excelled at: firing aimed shots faster and more accurately than the enemy, in any conditions. Though the weapons and equipment are constantly modernised (the Micks got the new design of helmets two years ago, the new rifles last year, and we are due the new webbing next year), Napoleon's generals would still have recognised the discipline and aggression, as would the Kaiser's, and Hitler's.

As the General's visit ended, the competition drew to a close. The Commanding Officer presented the prizes to the victorious 2 Company team, and we had finished with ISAAC 1989. The battalion boarded the vehicles to return to Chelsea Barracks, ceremonial duties – and Alice, of course.

Sergeant Twomey giving his platoon some gentle encouragement

CONNOR'S DAY

or

'It's a Dog's Life in the Irish Guards'

I woke as usual at half past six, and went straight out for a run in the park, like I do every morning, with LCpl Smith who has the bunk next to mine. We got back to the Barracks at a quarter past seven, and then I realised something strange was going on: I got some breakfast.

Now normally I am not allowed to eat breakfast, because of public (ceremonial) duties. The rest of the battalion is ordered to eat before parades – for if a man faints and he has missed breakfast, he can be charged with rendering himself unfit for duty. However, it is different for an Irish Wolfhound; they are all terribly worried that I'll have to answer nature's call along with the call of duty, and embarrass us all in some grand place like Wellington Barracks Square, or the Mall, or even the forecourt of Buckingham Palace. So on the days when I lead the Micks on Mounting Guards, I don't get breakfast, I just make up for it at lunch. On this particular Friday I remembered that of course all the men were away shooting ISAAC or some other unlucky fellow. (Humans do lead a terribly hard life sometimes.) What was more, not only did I have breakfast with the family (I live in the Smiths' Quarter in Chelsea Barracks) – toast, bacon and sausages, washed down with milk – but we had no muster parade that morning, and no Adjutant's Orders to attend. We usually go in daily, so that I can check that he's doing his job right. Apart from LCpl Smith, and my driver (I have my own Land-Rover), the Adjutant is really the one I work most closely with; we always seem to take part in the same parades, but we usually get back to barracks first, leaving the officers and men on guard.

With no Changing the Guard today, we had a lovely relaxed morning – a drive down to the Guards Depot to see a couple of my friends in the Guards Dog Unit – German Shepherd Guard Dogs. A run round the woods, and then pies and sandwiches for lunch.

My coat, like a bearskin, is well groomed but very thick and warm so I had my usual 'Irish siesta' in the afternoon. In fact I usually take things easy until I have dinner at seven with the Smiths. I have tripe and biscuits, except on Sundays when it's meat and two veg (and millions of spuds, of course). After dinner the people watch the television but I prefer to watch the tropical fish in the Smiths' tank: give me piranha fish any day over cricket or soap operas. At half past eight I have a final walk in Burton's Court, opposite the Royal Hospital Chelsea, and then I go to bed about eleven – hoping it's a breakfast day tomorrow.

Connor is the Irish Wolfhound (Mascot) of the
1st Battalion Irish Guards.

Myself and Lance-Corporal Smith

Germany

An Armoured Infantry Battalion: The Royal Scots

Mechanised infantry in battle. This chapter illustrates what it would be like, through the eyes of the Royal Scots.

Werl is a small, quiet West German pilgrimage town on the line of the historic Bundestrasse One. Napoleon marched through it on his way to Moscow, but today the road is used by those who wish to avoid the pressures of autobahn driving and see something of the pleasant, rolling countryside of Westphalia. Werl serves the prosperous Westphalian Plain as a market town. It lies on the eastern edge of the Ruhr coalfield and is some fifteen miles from the Möhne Dam, one of the targets of the famous 'Dambusters' raid. On the hills above the town, amongst cool, dark pines, is Albuhera Barracks, the present station for the 1st Battalion the Royal Scots.

The Royal Scots, the First of Foot, is the oldest regiment of the line in the British Army. Its ancestors served abroad from the 1630s onwards, and the tradition of foreign service continues today. The 1st Battalion is part of the 3rd Armoured Division, which is the 1st British Corps' reserve division. The division has the important task of defeating any enemy breakthrough into the British Corps area and is equipped with the Army's latest equipment, including the Warrior Armoured Infantry Fighting Vehicle.

Warrior is the replacement tracked vehicle for the now outdated FV 432. It weighs twenty-eight tonnes, carries ten men, and mounts a turret with a 30mm Rarden cannon and a 7.62mm chain gun. The crew comprises a commander and gunner, who sit in the turret, and a driver. All three remain with the vehicle. Seven infantrymen are carried in the back, forming the dismounting element. It is they who carry out the traditional infantry role of closing with and destroying the enemy. Powered by a 550bhp Perkins engine and fitted with an advanced suspension system, Warrior can move cross-country faster than any other armoured vehicle currently in service with the British Army. On roads it can reach speeds in excess of 45mph with ease. The vehicle provides increased armoured protection from artillery fire and certain anti-tank weapons for the soldiers it carries, and its special air filtration system enables the crew to survive closed-down inside the vehicle when nuclear, chemical and biological weapons have been used. Infantry battalions equipped with Warrior are known as armoured infantry.

The Royal Scots were the third infantry battalion in the Army to convert from the older FV 432 to Warrior. Tactical training with Warrior, following conversion, started in March 1989 with a series of map exercises and discussions. This was developed further during a deployment in the field to practise

battle procedures and enable the battalion to see just how mobile Warrior is. At 0300 hours on 30 June 1989, 1st Battalion the Royal Scots found itself deployed into hides, along with the attached tanks, artillery and engineers that make up the Royal Scots Battlegroup.

The previous day had been one of frantic activity. An earlier breakthrough by an enemy motor rifle division supported by tanks and artillery had been halted by 6th Armoured Brigade, of which the Royal Scots form a part. At 1800 hours on 28 June the brigade had been ordered to take three positions which formed a bridgehead from which the enemy could further develop his attack. It had been a difficult task. By last light the three armoured infantry companies of the Royal Scots were in defensive positions that were strongly held, although hastily prepared. Supported by Milan missile firing posts from the battlegroup's anti-tank platoon, and fire from the mortar platoon and the artillery, the companies held out against probing attacks by enemy reconnaissance patrols of armoured vehicles and tanks. In these short, sharp engagements, the night viewing sight that Warrior mounts came into its own. After reassessing the situation, however, the Brigade Commander decided to pull back the battlegroup and move it into temporary hides.

The soldiers had found it a long and tiring period. Once in the hides, sentries had been posted to protect the company positions, and many of the men took

Members of a Rifle Section stand ready for action in front of their Warrior Mechanised Combat Vehicles

the opportunity to get some rest, if only for a few minutes. In the quiet of the dawn, the young platoon commanders and their sergeants walked around the four vehicles that made up their command, to check their soldiers and their equipment. In the move between the last position and this, a number of the Jocks had taken the opportunity to make a hot drink, and as the chill of early morning crept into them, the sweet tea lifted their morale.

Whilst the enemy had probed the positions the Jocks held, it had managed also to break through once more to the north. The brigade that it faced had been forced to give ground. The pulling-back of 6th Armoured Brigade had given the Divisional Commander the force he needed to destroy the enemy. It appeared that the enemy force, consisting of two motor rifle regiments (the equivalent of a British brigade), plus a flank guard of a tank company, had halted seventeen kilometres to the north-west of the brigade's current position, and that they were facing south-west. The brigade's mission was to destroy the enemy, and the attack would begin at 0430 hours.

The armoured regiment of 6 Armoured Brigade had the task of piercing the enemy formation. This required the destruction of the tanks that formed the flank guard. Their attack would be supported by the full firepower of all available artillery batteries and mortars, and would be preceded by an attack by RAF Tornado and Harrier aircraft. Once through, the tanks would press on into the enemy's main body, preparing the way for the armoured infantry to clear any remaining opposition. It would be a bold attack, requiring determination and aggressive spirit to see it through. The speed of reaction of the whole brigade, and the use of maximum firepower to keep the enemy's heads down would be vital factors. Two important enemy locations had been identified as objectives for the Royals. One appeared to be an enemy headquarters, the other an area of high ground. As this information came into the command Warrior, the Company Commander called an orders group.

The Company Sergeant Major moved around the position, calling platoon commanders and those in charge of the elements attached to the Company Group. They assembled quickly to hear the brief set of orders that explained their respective tasks in the battle to come. The company was to be the right assault company in the battlegroup attack. It had the job of destroying the enemy headquarters. The fireplan would be under the control of the company once it moved from its final assault position on to the enemy position. As the Company Commander confirmed the final details of the movement plan, he stressed the need for speed of reaction and movement. There would be no room for indecision: the task had been detailed, everyone knew what his job was and how he fitted in.

The platoon commanders went back to their soldiers and covered the facts and details that affected their men. Equipment was checked once more and the Jocks paired off to arrange each other's camouflage. Once complete, the sections mounted their vehicles. Space is at a premium in the back of a Warrior. Seven men plus their personal equipment, rifles, LAW 80 anti-tank missiles, ammunition, rations, jerricans of water, sleeping bags, kit bags, and the vehicle tool kit soon fill the available space. However, without all this the infantry's most vital asset, the soldier, does not function effectively.

Soon the company moved off. The route had been marked by the reconnaissance platoon; even so, as they moved at speed past each key point vehicle commanders glanced at their maps to check their progress. It was important that the brigade did not move too far forward too soon. To do so would run the risk of compromising the most vulnerable part of the operation. Until the armoured regiment had crossed its start line, the armoured infantry would pause momentarily in forward holding areas. As the Warriors moved on, the section commanders continued to tell their men over the vehicle briefing system what they were to do and what they should expect.

The thirteen kilometres to the forward holding area were covered in as many minutes. The Second-in-Command organised the company into the final order of march whilst the other commanders carried out final checks. Already the tanks ahead were in action and it seemed as though they had made contact with, and destroyed the majority of the enemy flank guard. The effects of the artillery bombardment and the air strikes had been devastating. The enemy were caught off balance by the shock of the attack. The progress the tanks had made enabled the Commanding Officer to advance the timings for the move of his companies.

As radio silence was lifted on the company radio net, the Warriors started up and moved out as one. It was a further four kilometres to the final assault position, and, since the company group was complete, it was the Company Commander's intention to move straight through into the attack. As the group moved at best speed towards the start line, evidence of the recent tank battle littered the area. There were no problems on the move, and the Forward Observation Officer reported that the fireplan was ready. The Company Commander started his countdown.

As the company moved out, the fireplan started. Reports from the lead platoons indicated that the artillery fire was being most effective in keeping the enemy pinned down. The move across open ground involved covering about 1,500 metres, but, with the fireplan to cover the company, and with the

A Challenger Tank and a Warrior move forward together. Unlike its predecessors, Warrior is capable of keeping up with a Main Battle Tank across country

speed and protection the Warriors afforded, the company was certain it would get on to the objective unscathed. The vehicles were soon moving at top speed across the featureless landscape that surrounded the enemy's position. From the moment the lead vehicles broke cover, they could see the enemy headquarters, halted at the edge of a wood. In under a minute the company had hit its objective.

As the two forward platoons prepared to dismount, the chain guns clattered into action, covering the near edge of the enemy position with machine-gun fire. The platoon commanders barked their orders to dismount and the vehicles came to an abrupt standstill amongst the enemy. Following well-rehearsed dismounting drills, the riflemen poured out of the Warriors and in next to no time were providing their own fire support as the Warriors reversed away at high speed to give covering fire from positions where they would be less vulnerable to short-range anti-tank weapons.

By the time the Warriors had reached the objective, the riflemen in the back had been sufficiently aware of what was going on around them to know that their own survival would depend on the spirit of fight they could produce. When the power rear doors opened, the men moved out to the left and right of their vehicles, into their battle positions, and began to shoot at the enemy. Once the Warriors had reversed out of their way, the sections began to move forward to clear the enemy positions at bayonet point.

It was a long business. The Company Sergeant Major had difficulty in keeping the platoons resupplied with ammunition. As the two lead platoons secured their objectives, it looked as though the position was taken, but suddenly an enemy depth position sprang into life. Almost immediately, the Company Commander committed his third platoon, which had been kept in reserve for just such an eventuality. Using the fire provided by the now empty Warriors to support their move forward, the third platoon dashed forward and hit the enemy at full speed. In the face of all this, the enemy resistance collapsed.

Throughout the Royal Scots' positions, those enemy who had survived were breaking. After considering the situation, the Commanding Officer concluded that his training objectives had been achieved. Picking up the radio handset, he called the exercise to a halt. The battlegroup had been in the field for two weeks and had practised a number of operations of war. It was now time for him to call in his battlegroup to tell his men of their achievements.

Gathering the soldiers around him, the Commanding Officer explained what he had set out to achieve two weeks ago. The two weeks of training on the Soltau-Luneberg Training Area had given the Royal Scots the opportunity to test to the full those operating procedures and ideas that had been developed since the conversion to Warrior had started in the new year. Just as important, it had allowed the soldiers to practise their infantry skills in the field. 30 June 1989 was the culmination of the Royal Scots' battlegroup training. The battalion could now look forward to returning to Werl and the preparations for firing camp, when the Warriors' guns could be fired on the range. The vehicles started to move off to the washdown point and thence to the trains that would take them home.

The Corps of Royal Electrical and Mechanical Engineers: A Day in the Life of an Armoured Workshop

The modern Army depends on its increasingly complex equipment working properly. It is the job of the Royal Electrical and Mechanical Engineers to ensure that this happens.

'Hello 71, this is 13J, Taskrep, over', the radio crackles.

'71. Send, over.'

'13J, Serial 18 – ZAP 205, Serial 36 – Grid 822903 . . . over.'

Corporal Broadhead rapidly decodes the message and briefs his boss: 'The battlegroup have an armoured personnel carrier on the prairie north of Antelope Road with a blown engine – shall I call Corporal Bromby, it's his crew's turn for a task?'

At the British Army Training Unit Suffield (BATUS), not far from Calgary in western Canada, a detachment of twenty-five men from 6 Armoured Workshop's Forward Repair Group (FRG) is being kept busy looking after the 17/21st Lancers battlegroup engaged in Exercise Gazala, the climax of their live firing exercises.

'The B81 power pack is in the back of the stores truck, Corporal Bromby,' AQMS Williams explains, 'I've put the casualty's location and registration number on the Taskrep card; get away as soon as you can. Take Rattlesnake Road to the junction with Antelope Road. Then you'll need clearance before you enter the range template – it's being controlled on channel 4.'

*   *   *

Prior to going to BATUS, the battlegroups carried out two weeks' preparatory training in the Soltau Training Area in northern Germany. Although half of the FRG is in Canada for six weeks, most of the rest are supporting the Blues and Royals battlegroup on exercise in Soltau. It is 0300 hours in Munster, and the Workshop Duty Officer's phone rings at 6 Armoured Workshop Royal Electrical and Mechanical Engineers' base in West Germany.

'Morning, sir, it's Sergeant Richards, ringing from Soltau. Sorry to wake you at this hour but we've had a host of tasks during the night. We've already lifted two Challenger CV12 power packs and once we've fitted new ones, I'll have no fit stock left. The battlegroup have already warned me of a third tank needing a new pack and the Commanding Officer wants everything fit for his final exercise tomorrow. I know you've got none fit in Munster at the moment, but hopefully the lads in the Power Pack Section can make something of the ones we've just lifted. They should be with you in about an hour. . . .'

Trying to establish why a component snapped

'Another glorious Canadian sunset,' Lieutenant Robinson, the FRG commander in BATUS, observes as he enters the FRG command post. 'Brief me on the latest situation, please, "Q".'

'It's been a fairly quiet day. Corporal Baber and his two crew are on their way here having fitted an L60 in one of C Squadron's Chieftains. Corporal Fincham and his men are resting – they haven't had a task since they changed the final drive in one of Recce Troop's Scorpions this morning. Corporal Bromby's team are on task north of the Antelope Road changing a B81 – they should be finished in about three hours.'

'Good, live firing's just stopped and if the last few nights are anything to go by, we'll be hearing from the battlegroup soon, once their own fitters have had a chance to check out the day's casualties.'

*   *   *

Only an hour later, in Munster, Buller Barracks is coming to life as the soldiers and civilians employed in the workshop start work. Although most of the FRG are in Canada or Soltau, this is only one small part of 6 Armoured Workshop. Commanded by a major, it has about 250 officers and soldiers, organised into six platoons, and employs over seventy German civilians. By 0800 hours, most of the repair shops are humming as the tradesmen set about their various repair tasks. In 'B' Shop, the overhead crane is sweeping down with a new Bedford axle. In 'A' Shop, Corporal Tait and his crew of two vehicle mechanics have been hard at work for three hours; having inspected and confirmed that a new engine is needed, they are well on their way to having the first CV12 pack stripped apart. Unfortunately life is never simple – the Stores Platoon confirms that they have no Challenger engines in stock and that the next one is not expected for three or four days; improvisation will obviously be needed if the Blues and Royals are to have all their tanks working.

At 0900 hours the weekly production conference is being brought to order by Major Rod Paul, who runs the civilian labour force and doubles as the workshop's Production Officer. He's assisted by the Artificer Sergeant Major – the ASM.

'First, ASM, can you give us a summary of last week's activities?'

'Yes, in total the workshop repaired ten power packs, thirty-two vehicles and ninety-four assorted electronic and optical items. In particular, we fixed the last four of those fuel tankers that have been awaiting gearbox spares. In terms of productive hours, we've achieved 2,320 hours, excluding all the work done in Canada and Soltau.'

'What about new work received in the last week?'

'Well, 14/20th Hussars came back off exercise with a lot of dead equipment and 2nd Field Regiment has just finished a major inspection in preparation for firing camp starting in three weeks. The result is that we've received over 3,000 hours of new work, and most of this is on priority jobs. And, finally, we received two more dead CV12 power packs from the FRG at Soltau a few hours ago.'

'We'll discuss tackling that lot later, once the platoon commanders have given me their expected manpower availability for the next week. . . .'

*   *   *

'Well, it's a bit warmer here in Canada than it was in Soltau in March.' Craftsman Dale appears, streaked in oil, from the depths of the engine compartment where he has been tightening up a mounting bolt. 'Another half hour should see this job finished; we should be back at the FRG asleep by first light. Let's have a sup of that coffee, Taff.'

'Hello 71D, this is 71, send SITREP, over.'

A line-up of Warrior Mechanised Combat Vehicles in Germany

07FD41

'71D, about thirty minutes to completion if there are no problems, over,' replies Corporal Bromby, clambering on to his vehicle. Two minutes later, he jumps down again. 'No sleep for us tonight. That was the boss; all the other crews are already on task and D Squadron needs a new gearbox in one of its Chieftains - it's about six miles from here so they're sending out a truck with the spares and we're to meet it there.'

'Never mind, only six days to R & R [Rest and Recuperation],' muses Craftsman Dale. 'I'm off canoeing in the Rockies for a fortnight with Mr Robinson. You're going back after the normal four days, aren't you, Taff?'

'Yes,' replies Craftsman Browne, 'but I'm going to make the most of it - Geordie and I are going to hire a car and drive into the States to visit Yellowstone Park, getting back in time to spend a night in the Cadillacs Club in Medicine Hat. . . .'

A Platoon Commander plans the next move from the turret of his Warrior

A Scimitar tracked armoured reconnaissance vehicle which mounts a 30mm Rarden cannon. The four short barrels on each forward edge of the turret are smoke dischargers arranged in such a pattern as to form an instant smokescreen in front of the vehicle in an emergency

*   *   *

83

It is just after lunch when the phone rings in Captain Rob Tuck-Brown's office. 'Sir, can you come across to the Gun Shop? I think we've found a serious defect which could affect the Warrior fleet.' Five minutes later the Platoon Commander and the Weapons Artificer are studying the bits of broken and twisted metal.

'We took this out of a Warrior in Oxford Barracks this morning – they had been practising firing at multiple targets, using the power traverse, when suddenly the turret went out of control – it's a good job they weren't live firing on the range or someone could have been killed. What appears to have happened is. . . .'

Between them they must decide whether this is a one-off fault or whether other vehicles are likely to be affected, and if the defect is likely to endanger life.

Fifteen minutes later: 'I'll leave you to dig out the part numbers and the vehicle details, Staff. I'm going to brief Major Lower that we should recommend the whole fleet be grounded at least until we've had time to get this examined in detail and to inspect a few more.'

The Officer Commanding, Major Mike Lower, is putting down the phone as Captain Tuck-Brown knocks and enters. 'That was the FRG from Soltau – they've cleared most of the tasks from last night, less a Chieftain power pack change that's in hand and one badly bogged tank – they're having to find a route in for a second armoured recovery vehicle, and, of course, the last Challenger pack change – how are the lads doing on those packs that came in this morning?'

'We've been slowed down by the lack of a new engine but we've found a good engine in the second pack they sent us – it needs a couple of hours of work on minor jobs, but if everything goes well we should have something ready for out-inspection later this afternoon. But that's not why I came across – Staff Sergeant MacDonald has found a potential major problem. . . .'

Back in the power pack repair bay, Corporal Tait and his crew are still working as first the civilians and then the soldiers finish their day's tasks and return home. 'We'll take a quick break for some tea and then we should be ready to run it up in another hour,' he briefs Captain Tuck-Brown, who has come across to check on progress before going home for the day.

'The Duty Officer will organise a truck as soon as you've finished and you know my home number if there are any problems.'

It is 1900 hours when the peace of the evening is broken by the cough of the Challenger engine being fired into life by its starter motors, soon followed by the roar of the twenty-six-litre engine and the scream of the twin turbos. Corporal Tait busies around the pack checking for oil leaks and tightening the odd bolt; ten minutes later the crew are smiling as they clear up, looking forward to a well-deserved shower.

The Duty Officer, having dispatched the still warm power pack to Soltau, is settling down to a quiet evening when the phone rings: 'Corporal Johnson, Military Police, sir. We've got a job for your duty recovery crew – there's been an accident on the autobahn ten miles north of Munster. There's an eight-tonne on its side – can you get someone up there as soon as possible?'

It is approaching midnight in Munster when the recovery crew return to conclude another busy day for the workshop. Meanwhile in Canada:

'Hello 71, this is 13J, Taskrep, over.' The radio crackles in the FRG command post.

'I suppose it was too much to expect a quiet afternoon,' Corporal Broadhead comments as he answers the call. Minutes later, Corporal Bromby and his crew are loading up in the Alberta sunshine.

'It's a Chieftain auxiliary generator about eight miles down Bayonet Trail,' he briefs his crew. 'Let's hope we get back before first light this time.'

A CVI2 Challenger Tank Power Pack being fine tuned by REME fitters. A power pack can be changed in the field, although it is a complex and time-consuming operation

85

Battle casualty simulation can
be quite realistic on exercise!
(see previous chapter)

A Chieftain Power Pack change
in progress

A badly bogged Challenger tank
about to be extricated

Building Bridges with 28 Amphibious Engineer Regiment

Captain D J G Wood RE

The Royal Engineers are responsible, amongst many things, for getting the rest of the Army across rivers. The Amphibious Engineer Regiment forms a vital part of BAOR.

The peace in the harbour area was undisturbed, except for the insistent and mildly annoying buzz of flies. The Troop Commander thought that they were probably flying round the same small area in a patch of strong sunlight to keep warm; the Troop Staff Sergeant opined that there was probably something nasty buried beneath the carpet of dead leaves. The Clansman radio in the Sultan Command Vehicle squeaked into life with a request for a Critical Asset Return and a Warning Order for a task, sent in BATCO radio code.

The critical assets being referred to were the twelve M2D Amphibious Bridging and Ferrying Vehicles operated by the troop, which lay dispersed and camouflaged under the high oak and pine trees of this wooded harbour area, about thirty kilometres south-east of Hamburg. The M2, or Alligator as it is known in West German service, is a vehicle the size of an average forty-five-seater passenger coach, and is essentially a self-propelled bridging pontoon. It consists of a boat-like main hull and two outrigger pontoons, or side-swimmers, which are lifted hydraulically to rest on top for road travel and which are extended and lowered to the sides for stability on the water. These vehicles, or 'rigs' as they are normally called, were just some of those in use with 28 Amphibious Engineer Regiment on that stifling June afternoon, and the troop was nearing the end of a three-week Commanding Officer's Exercise.

Whilst the signaller busied himself with decoding the latest message from on high, the Troop Commander's mind raced back over a fairly hectic three weeks, which had taken the troop from Hameln (of Pied Piper fame), the regiment's home base on the River Weser, eastwards to the River Leine and north to the River Aller, before swinging north-west to the mouth of the Weser in the Bremerhaven area. They had then moved once more east, in the early hours of yesterday morning, to their present location not far short of the Inner German Border. In that time, the sixty men had adjusted to the soldiers' normal routine of work at night and lie-up during the day. They had carried out a large number of ferrying and bridging operations, in addition to the more usual Engineer jobs of demolitions and dry bridging using the Medium Girder Bridge. For part of the time they had been in support of another Engineer regiment for joint river crossing operations, and on one occasion had carried infantrymen over a one-kilometre-wide stretch of the Weser, using their rigs as landing craft.

'It's a Warning Order for a bridge across the River Elbe, sir,' said the Signaller.

'Can't be right,' said Staff; 'the Elbe is miles wide.'

'A bit less than that,' mused the Troop Commander, 'but by the map it's about two hundred and fifty to three hundred metres and a damn sight wider than we're used to. Ask them to confirm that they do mean we've got to bridge as opposed to ferrying.'

The confirmation came within seconds, along with details of the Orders Group, at which the Commanding Officer would give his instructions for this, the longest M2 bridge built by the regiment in recent years. The bridge was to be built across the river at Lauenburg, and at that point it was some two hundred and thirty metres wide, which would require a minimum of thirty-two rigs to complete. It was to be built and ready for traffic by 0030 hours the following morning.

While the Troop Commander attended the 'O' Group in Regimental Headquarters, which was ensconced in yet another fly's paradise of a farmyard some twenty-five kilometres away, the remainder of the troop were roused from their fitful dozing in the late afternoon sunshine to prepare their main compo meal of the day, check equipment and attend to the usual rituals of washing, shaving and boot and weapon cleaning.

Each rig crew comprises a driver, who drives the vehicle on land, a pilot, who operates it when it becomes a 'boat' on the water, and the youngest member, a crewman, who operates the hydraulic ramp controls and does all the deck jobs. The commander, who is typically a twenty-three-year-old Lance-Corporal, makes up the four-man crew. Usually the most experienced crew member, and an Amphibious Engineer Class One, he can do all of the others' jobs, and if the crew is reduced to three, due to manpower shortages or a temporary absence, he normally also drives. Amphibious Engineer is an additional trade to Combat Engineer, and many of the men also have an artisan trade, such as plumber, draughtsman or sheet metal worker, as a third string.

In harbour the rig is usually opened out to its full water width of six metres, and the four independently suspended wheels can be retracted into the main hull, so that it appears to squat on the ground. This means that its shape is changed considerably as an aid to camouflage, and the crew can gain access to the main hull and engines for essential servicing and checks. It also has the added advantage that, by spreading a canopy over the on-board crane, a shelter can be made in which to sleep and cook when in harbour.

As the afternoon turned into a slightly cooler early evening, each crew methodically checked over their rig. Each of the two big Magirus Deutz diesel engines was inspected, along with all the operating controls, the propulsion system, including the big main propeller, and the myriad parts of the hydraulic system. The crane, for moving the ramps which connected the rigs together and the inshore rig to the beach, was tested for free operation. The main hull and its two sideswimmers, with their secondary propellers, were carefully scrutinised. Oil levels were topped up and minor repairs carried out. The worst damage to hulls etc. had been reported on arrival in the area after last

A general view of a REME repair shop (see previous chapter)

night's operation, and the troop's attached REME Forward Repair Team had worked on for hours after most others had taken to their sleeping bags.

One by one the Corporals who commanded each rig section reported their charges ready for the water. On full fuel tanks of five hundred litres, each rig has a road range of one thousand kilometres, or can operate in river current speeds of two metres a second (about four knots) for about six and a half hours without refuelling. Three joined together can form a ferry capable of carrying the Challenger tank, or they can be coupled to form a bridge capable of carrying even the heaviest Army loads. All that remained to be done by seven that evening was to attend the Troop Commander's Orders or 'O' Group, and at last light dismantle the camouflage net, close up and move to the river.

At the 'O' Group held on the Troop Commander's return, each Rig Commander was briefed on his part in the forthcoming operation, his place in bridge and on the contingency plans in case of breakdown, accident or enemy interference. All five troops of the regiment would be involved, with twenty-eight rigs in bridge and at least a further six in reserve. Safety cover was to be provided by combat support boats from the Support Squadron.

At prearranged intervals that night, the troop columns left their widely dispersed harbour and hide areas and, following the regimental route, after a twenty-kilometre drive arrived at the bridge site in the carefully thought-out launching order. Under a slightly overcast sky, but with a fair amount of ambient light and a touch of red to the west to show where the sun had expired, the safety boats, their navigation lights brightly lit for the occasion, skittered about like playful sheepdogs before settling down to hold station in midstream. They were to stay on the alert for any soldier unlucky enough to go overboard. As each group of rigs arrived they moved quietly on to the sloping cobbled ramp, which in times past had been used by a civilian ferry, and with a hiss of hydraulics opened out. The crew, moving rapidly yet almost soundlessly, carried out the few jobs required to convert the land vehicle to a boat, and within seconds the rigs slid rapidly into the dark water and powered away to swing out

A chance to show the flag!

their ramps and couple together in twos and threes. Simultaneously the men of the bank support section tugged and pulled their steel wire ropes and tirfor winches into place, to provide anchorages from which to hold the ends of the bridge in the correct depth of water for loading.

Within a few minutes all the rigs had arrived and splashed in, and the earlier arrivals which had formed two- and three-rig rafts were crabbing across the river and pushing upstream to the bridge centreline. The crane ratchets of the later arrivals could still be heard clearly as their crews outramped, and rising bow waves could be spotted as an occasional laggard powered upstream to its proper place in the echelon. Both the two-rig landing bays had moved into the banks on the centreline, and their combined crews, assisted by the ubiquitous bank support section, had connected the anchor ropes and the short ramp sections, which were added to the main ramps to allow traffic easy access to the bridge.

The Troop Staff Sergeant detailed to supervise the construction was insistently calling the rafts into the head of the bridge, where they coupled on with remarkable rapidity. The end of the bridge was clearly visible as it grew out of the far bank, and needed only a couple of rafts to make it complete. At that moment the men detailed as River Watchers radioed that a fast-moving vessel was coming downstream, and the Safety Officer, not at all sure of the newcomer's identity or intentions, fired an illuminating parachute flare over the nearly complete bridge to warn of the obstruction across its bows. The *Wasserschutz Polizei*, or River Police launch, whose arrival had been expected much earlier, turned on its blue flashing light and jauntily turned to take station upstream, in order to intercept any barge or ship choosing to ignore the river closure order which had been imposed by the river authorities for the night.

Finally, the closure raft inched carefully into the remaining gap, and after the briefest hesitation the ramps dropped into their receiving lugs and were pinned. The bridge was complete, the air blowers on each rig whined as the remaining air bags were inflated for additional buoyancy, and footwalk posts and ropes were installed. A few last checks by the Bridge Commander, and it was declared ready for traffic, seven minutes ahead of time. The first vehicles loomed out of the darkness on the south bank, driving only on convoy lights with each one following the barely seen, under-chassis-mounted, single white light of the one in front. Rig Commanders stationed on the inshore ramp guided the drivers on with brief flashes of their green lights, and the convoy drove steadily across. The bridge was held against the current by the engine power of twenty-eight port engines, finely adjusted by the pilots on their stands above the rig cabs. From the start to finish, the bridge had taken under three hours to build. It remained in place only a few minutes more, when the Commanding Officer ordered not only a change of the command team which had built it, but a change of design as well. The bridge was to be broken, more rigs were to be added to reduce the water gaps between them, and the whole thing reassembled within one hour.

Following only a little chaos, much speedy uncoupling and in-ramping, and a very occasional one-sided angry conversation between 'Staff' and a couple of

luckless young sappers, the aim was achieved, and shortly after the break of a glorious dawn, each rig ran the Union Flag up its mast in honour of a very rare occasion. Bridge lengths vary from three to four rigs on the Leine to an average ten rigs on the Weser and really, given the practised excellence of the crews, this last thirty-one-rig bridge of Exercise Neptune's Gallop 1989 should not have aroused much emotion, but it did made the thirtieth of June a little bit different.

The completed bridge made up of Royal Engineer M2 floating rigs. Such a bridge would normally be dismantled before dawn in wartime since it would be a prime target for enemy aircraft during daylight hours. An M2 bridge is capable of taking the Challenger Main Battle Tank

The Royal Military Police in Berlin

An East German border guard making a video from on top of the Berlin Wall. He chose an ironic slogan to sit above!

The situation in Berlin has undergone massive changes recently. But the Four Powers are likely to remain responsible for the city for the foreseeable future. The Royal Military Police role in the city is particularly important. Captain Richard Moore is Adjutant and British Sector Operations Officer with 2nd Regiment Royal Military Police. He has served in Berlin for three years.

'Hello, Romeo 24 Bravo, this is Zero. Go now to directly north of the Reichstag. West Berlin Police report an escape.'

It is 0100 hours on 30 June 1989. An RMP patrol is tasked to the scene of an escape from the Soviet Sector of Berlin. On arrival the patrol members find that two men have apparently just crashed a lorry through a fence and swum across the River Spree. They are now both gratefully sipping piping hot coffee, provided by RMP, still dripping wet, with looks of wonderment and happiness written across their faces.

Berlin. A city divided by ideologies. The 'last outpost of freedom', over one hundred miles from West Germany and only forty miles from the Polish border. The British Army with a garrison of 3,000 troops maintains Britain's 'protective presence' here, behind the Iron Curtain. An island surrounded by 165 kilometres of wire and wall complete with barren expanses, blinding searchlights, war dogs, and sinister guard towers. A city containing such famous (and infamous) landmarks as Hitler's Bunker, the Reichstag, the 'Wall' and the Soviet War Memorial. A place where the legacy of the Second World War still rests upon the shoulders of the British, French and American Allies forty-five years later and where the effects of post-war decisions impact on the daily routine of the RMP soldiers. The role of the 2nd Regiment of the Royal Military Police is unique. It is only in Berlin that dealings with Russian soldiers from the Soviet Sector are commonplace; simply day-to-day duties.

Captain Richard Moore's day begins as the ring of the telephone wakes him with a start from a deep sleep. It is Sergeant Eddie Grant at the RMP Control Room, warning him of a possible major problem in the Soviet Sector. The time must be around 0130 hours. A group of soldiers have gone across to East Berlin for an evening's entertainment. All servicemen must return to the West before 0030 hours, but tonight only five out of the group of six are back on time at Checkpoint Charlie; one has got lost along the way. A patrol is already searching, and other mobiles are on stand-by.

There are only a few places where he can be, but it isn't until 0500 hours that he is found walking along Unter den Linden, the most famous and beauti-

94

ful of Berlin's pre-war streets, having apparently lost contact with his friends. Panic over.

Having got back to bed for a few hours, at 0800 Captain Moore arrives at his office in the RMP Headquarters, which is housed in the 1936 Olympic Stadium Barracks, and by mid-morning is feeling a bit smug about the noticeable dent in the paperwork on his desk. Still outstanding is the project of redrafting the regulations for Autobahn Corridor travel, but that will have to wait. More pressing is the statistical report on British military travellers to the Soviet Sector last month: 7,874 travellers in June, an increase of over 2,000 on the same month last year. The trend is ever upwards, as East Berlin draws more and more visitors.

It is now 0915 hours. Down in the control room a shift change took place an hour ago, and a different platoon is now thinly dispersed throughout the British Sector of Berlin. Woman Corporal Debbie Burns and Corporal John Harvey make up today's Wall patrol. They are based at a duty room outside the Soviet War Memorial in the Tiergarten, tasked with policing the 3.7 kilometres of Wall which separates the British and Soviet sectors.

The Soviet War Memorial is one of only two places where the Russian military have representtion in the West, and in order to maintain it they employ soldiers who cross the Wall from their barracks in East Berlin. The Soviet soldiers guarding the Memorial are driven in every day, but because of the

Tank transporters from 16 Tank Transporter Squadron RCT on the final part of their journey into Berlin bringing 15th/19th Hussars' tanks to relieve the resident Cavalry Squadron

sometimes unpredictable reactions of West Berliners to the sight of Russian soldiers, 2 RMP are charged with escorting the guard when in transit. Although not a difficult duty, it is intriguing, and develops an unusual working relationship with the Soviets.

By 1030 hours the Wall patrol has completed its escort task and is free to assist an Engineer Corporal who has just had a collision in his car with an East German in the Soviet Sector. To reach East Berlin they must cross through Checkpoint Charlie, not far from their outpost. After dropping their weapons off – the RMP do not go armed into the Soviet Sector – with the Checkpoint Duty NCO, they arrive at the accident shortly after a *Volkspolizei* (People's Police) patrol has turned up. Under the Quadripartite Agreement for Berlin the East German Police have no jurisdiction over any of the three Western Powers, though they often try to assert their authority by demanding that soldiers produce identity documents. In this case the Corporal has refused, and an argument is in progress. W/Cpl Burns informs the *Volkspolizei* that their request is outside the terms of the Agreement, and that if they want any details they must call for a Soviet officer, to whom the information will be given. Avoiding further confrontation, the East Germans release the British soldier without further incident, other than contacting his insurance company the next day.

On the way back to their Wall patrol route, Debbie and John come across Mr John Runnings, a seventy-two-year-old American who travels to Berlin every summer to protest about the Wall. In 1986 he smashed a concrete top section of the Wall with a sledgehammer, and was arrested by East German Border Guards for his pains. He has returned to Potsdamer Platz – the Piccadilly Circus of old Berlin – meticulously to paint the part of the Wall which replaced the part he previously damaged.

The NCOs take no action – Wall graffiti is an acceptable activity in Berlin – other than to warn him that he runs the risk of being arrested by the East Germans again. For the purpose of upkeep the Wall was built approximately three metres east of the true border, creating a strip of land called the *Unterbaugebiet*. It is here, in what is technically the Soviet Sector, that civilians run the risk of being arrested by East German soldiers who can easily cross the Wall (when on duty) through one of several camouflaged doors. As far as they are concerned, the strip of land is not Soviet Sector but DDR territory, part of their 'Haupstadt' (capital city). The three Western Allies don't agree with the East Germans on this point, which has been the cause of many disagreements in the past.

Today's town patrols have not been very busy, but as it is hot and it's summer, they aren't too concerned. Patrolling the Ku-damm in the heart of West Berlin isn't exactly a hardship. Two patrols are out, one on motorcycles and the other in a standard duty van. The weather convinces these men to take the opportunity for a walk around the area of the war-damaged Kaiser Wilhelm Memorial Church, which is preserved as a constant reminder of the past. This area is always full of interest: mime artists, solo guitarists and full-blown jazz bands entertain the passing public. Contributions from the RMP are gladly received.

After lunch a town patrol is called to meet up with today's 'Wire' patrol at Gatow Ranges. Patrols of the forty kilometres of wire separating the British Sector from East Germany are performed by soldiers from the three resident infantry battalions and the Berlin Armoured Squadron, although until 1982 RMP carried out this task. Gatow Ranges are adjacent to the Wire, not far from Berlin's Royal Air Force Station.

Periodically, groups of East German soldiers cross over the Wire, laden with cameras to watch and photograph British soldiers shooting on the ranges. As is required by operating procedures, the Wire Patrol Commander from the 1st Battalion the King's Regiment has contacted the RMP regarding today's large presence of East Germans. The five soldiers prove, as always, to be quite a spectacle for passing motorists. No action is needed today as they are not encroaching into the British Sector. They do, however, offer a marvellous photographic opportunity for all the British soldiers present.

The Allied Checkpoint Charlie building. Once the only route that Allied personnel could use to travel into the Soviet Sector, with the dismantling of the wall it is now redundant

On training today are the men and women of 2 Platoon. Corporal Steve Giles has somehow talked his Platoon Commander into letting him go on a familiarisation helicopter flight around the Sector perimeter. Helicopter trips around the city are fascinating and great fun; they are an integral part of daily patrolling of the British Sector.

Two other members of the platoon have drawn the short straw, and are now dressed in their best uniforms to perform the once-monthly guard duties at the Allied Kommandatura building. The remainder of the platoon has been 'volunteered' to help the 1st Battalion the Black Watch with specialised training for fighting in built-up areas. The NCOs – all Military Policemen hold the rank of at least Lance-Corporal – join soldiers from other units in the garrison to play 'locals' in the Army training area of Ruhleben. This unusual experience turns out to be informative and fun. The time spent getting to know other Berlin servicemen away from the more common disciplined environment is good for both sides, and helps to generate a good relationship between the police and the military community.

At 2200 hours Captain Moore has to be at Checkpoint Bravo to receive a military convoy that has transitted East Germany along the road corridor from Helmstedt in the West. Already waiting are Sergeant Tosh Collins, RMP Sector Operations Sergeant, and Colour Sergeant Taff Skuse, a Royal Regiment of Wales soldier and one of seven Russian interpreters belonging to 2 RMP. Colour Sergeant Skuse has already driven down to the Soviet Checkpoint, one kilometre away in East Germany, to warn the Russians that a British military convoy is expected to enter the city. The convoy has already been through a Soviet Checkpoint at Marienborn on the West/East German border, where the numbers of men and vehicles have been thoroughly checked. The RMP's job, along with the Soviet Checkpoint Commander, at the end of the journey is to confirm the numbers have not increased due to any unauthorised hitch-hikers. A miscount necessitates a recount, and it is imperative that the numbers are accurate. The rapport between the British RMP and the Russians is excellent, and during the check conversation flows freely. There will no doubt be an excuse for them to drink vodka together again soon.

Upon completing their goodbyes, the convoy is led out of the Soviet Checkpoint, past numerous East German barriers, gates and armed border guards, whose task it is to keep their own people from entering West Berlin. It passes under a bridge, on the reverse of which is written the ominous words 'YOU ARE LEAVING THE AMERICAN SECTOR'. The RMP can now go home.

It has been a long day, but there are still a couple of hours to run, and this is Berlin, where anything can happen.

'Hello, Romeo 11 Alpha, this is Zero. We have an unconfirmed report of shots fired in the area of Brandenburg Gate. West Berlin Police are at the scene and have requested your assistance. . . .'

Northern Ireland

In Northern Ireland with the Royal Hampshires

The British Army has an appallingly difficult job to do in Northern Ireland, none more so than the Infantry. This chapter describes a day in the life of the Royal Hampshire Regiment, in this strife-torn corner of the United Kingdom.

The 1st Battalion the Royal Hampshire Regiment took over operational control of the city of Londonderry on 5 March 1989. The last time the 'Tigers' patrolled these streets was exactly ten years earlier. Then our Commanding Officer commanded Y Company, the Regimental Sergeant Major was a platoon Sergeant, and the majority of today's soldiers were just starting their secondary schools in Hampshire. The regiment is on a two-and-a-half year tour, so we have moved here with our families. The wives (but not the men) shop in the city, as they would anywhere in England. The children attend the local schools, where they are completely integrated and speak very highly of the educational standards.

The thirtieth of June was a fairly typical day. B Company were in the city for their second tour, A Company were training, and Y Company were committed to guards and duties. Z Company were just returning from a fortnight's well-earned leave while, as always, HQ Company were administering, paying, feeding, clothing and transporting the rest of the battalion.

But it is in the city, on the west bank of the River Foyle, that we shall concentrate, with the officers and men of B Company. Theirs was the first company to deploy into the city in March and now, halfway through their second tour, their knowledge of the ground and the way of life of Derry is unsurpassed. The following passages have been written by two of the platoon commanders.

*   *   *

Lieutenant S is twenty-five. A graduate in Geography from the University of Edinburgh, he was commissioned in the Argyll and Sutherland Highlanders three years ago. He has been attached to the Royal Hampshires since December last year. He commands 4 Platoon and has completed one city tour at RUC Rosemount, a detached platoon base close to the Creggan and Bogside areas of the city. This tour he is based in Fort George, alongside Company Headquarters.

Midnight passing marks the start of another day, and for many people the start of a good night's sleep. However, it also marks another six hours of duty for the sangar sentries and two teams on military escorts. The Platoon Commander

100

visits the sangars during the night, and is not surprised by the sentries' alertness and cheerfulness. On his way round, via the Operations Room, he hears about the armed escort vehicles in hot pursuit of a police Hotspur Land-Rover, which in turn is giving chase to an orange Lada for minor motoring offences. Other minor infringements, vehicle checkpoints (VCPs) and house calls keep the military escorts busy all night, but routine in the sangars seems endless. At 0600 hours, duties change. Two fresh teams start as the Quick Reaction Force, or QRF, which are changed regularly during the day. The QRF are pleased to hear that lunch is at Strand Road, where the food is better, and the two teams deploy with letters to write and books to read. Anything to break the monotony of waiting, yet being at a split second's notice to move, to any incident, anywhere in the city. Nothing happens.

A patrol at 1100 hours, involving three bleary-eyed teams, deploys into the city. Coffee and a careful briefing make the difference, and the boys spark as always. Vehicles are checked, dustbins avoided, sighting reports sent, car trawls and information reports filled out. As usual, nothing dramatic to report, but a quick and thorough debrief means no information is wasted.

Four teams deploy in pairs for a VCP task. VCPs are set apparently at random, and vehicles stopped in the same way, but there is a method in the madness. 'Oh no, not again,' remarks an attractive blonde whose car is stopped for the second time in a day. However, she leaves more cheerfully after a few choice words from one of the boys suggesting that her photograph should be changed because it doesn't do her justice.

After the evening meal four teams again deploy, accompanied by an RUC liaison officer, who is as helpful and cheerful as ever. Patrol tasks include keeping a particular lookout for flat-bed lorries, which are used by the IRA as baseplates for their inaccurate and random, but nonetheless effective, homemade mortars.

2045 hours, and the last patrol of the day has just left. Information in the briefing includes who is going where tonight, and various vehicles to be searched if the opportunity arises. The QRF is changed for the final time, and the boys get to bed.

2200 hours, and military escorts change. Midnight approaches, and those not on duty are fast asleep. A blast is heard outside the camp. Tension mounts. 'Contact wait out!' The confusion is exacerbated by differing reports on Police and Army radios. A Police vehicle has been hit. Tyre blown off. No one injured. The military escort team, commanded by a young corporal known to his friends as 'Flat Top', swings into action. The QRF are deployed. Seconds of confusion quickly change to clear-cut orders and a follow-up. Flat Top, Mac and Taff tear down an alley. Sadly, nothing is found. The area is cordoned. Midnight passes and another sleepless night begins.

*   *   *

Lieutenant F, also twenty-five, hails from Wales. Having served three years with the TA, he transferred to the Regular Army three years ago, and although from the Royal Regiment of Wales now sports the Royal Hampshire cap badge for his six-month attachment. He commands 5 Platoon at RUC Rosemount.

The sky was turning several shades of blue as night gave way to day. The first rays of the sun appeared over the stark metal mortar sheeting covering the cookhouse

The three teams stood shivering in the courtyard, shaking the chill of the morning from their bodies. We deployed on to the cold, deserted streets, two teams from the back gate and one from the front. In the gardens the grass glistened with dew, which left imprints where the soldiers' feet had passed. Each team was well aware of the danger that lurked on the seemingly innocent roads. At 0430 there are no civilians about, and if a bomb had been planted this would be an ideal time to detonate it.

Forty minutes later, having checked out several vehicles which were unknown to us, the teams re-entered the base. Another patrol complete. It is, as the Lance-Corporal says, 'a good way to start the day'.

Prior to the patrol I had been given a verbal briefing on the night's events. Now I return and read the log, paying particular attention to any changes in tasks or 'fast balls' for the forthcoming day.

While we have been patrolling the chef has been woken, and breakfast awaits our return. After breakfast I take a stroll around the base checking that

On patrol in Northern Ireland. Whilst one man moves the other covers him

all the daily administrative tasks have been completed. The ablutions, cookhouse and accommodation are checked for cleanliness, these jobs being a major headache in a platoon location. Once I am happy, the men are allowed to stand down until the next patrol. I use the words 'stand down' loosely. All teams are at ten minutes' notice to move.

As the day progresses the next task is a neighbourhood patrol with the RUC. I have found the attitude of the people in Londonderry surprising. Since our first tour, people will now talk to us first, and some will even stop for a chat. It is a shame, however, that they want nothing to do with the RUC. The briefing for the patrol will take place at Fort George, so all the teams jump on the vehicles and drive down. On arrival I have a chat with the Duty Sergeant, who hands me a map with a route or 'beat' on it. Once my men are fully briefed we move out on task.

Communication is the most important part of any patrol. It enables the Commander to maintain a mental picture of the location of any team, and to think how he would react if an incident occurred to any one of them.

Once the task is complete we return to Fort George and drop off the RUC. My vehicles are then sent to fuel up and also to collect our rations. Meanwhile

Members of 4 Platoon, B Company, of the Royal Hampshires carrying out a vehicle check in the city centre

I've walked into the Ops Room to find the Ops Officer with his feet on his desk eating Smarties, thinking about an Op order he is due to write.

Having collected the mail and picked up the following day's patrol tasks, the vehicles arrive and we return to Rosemount for lunch.

An afternoon patrol is on the task sheet – providing a reassuring presence on the ground, and an opportunity for gathering intelligence and seeing who is about. It is not easy for any of us to stop and chat to people that we do not know, but in time confidence grows. As we move on from chatting to some cheerful and cheeky young kids with an impressive vocabulary (even to a soldier), they throw a few stones at us and run away laughing. They are only doing what their brothers and sisters have done before them, and in some cases probably their parents. Returning to camp the debrief reveals an interesting sighting of a suspected IRA member, but this information on its own is of little significance, as there is no evidence to link him to a crime. Administration takes up much of the day, especially if there are a lot of patrols. But the days flash by in a blur.

We are able to stand down for a while in the evening to get some sleep, write letters, play darts or watch TV. I spend some time extracting the following day's tasking for my platoon and allocate teams to each task. Any problems within the platoon are dealt with; my door is always open for a chat, and there is always someone with a problem.

Another patrol completes the evening. On return a bath, and a final word with the Guard Commander, whom I ask not to wake me up unless something goes 'bang'. Then it's time to slide into bed for a few hours' sleep, to be woken once again for a patrol that will signal the start of a new day.

*   *   *

Twenty-four hours have indeed passed, but the end of a day does not necessarily mean sleep. In each of the bases a guard goes on duty. The Company Operations Room is manned by a signaller, and a watchkeeper keeping abreast of all patrolling activity by Police and Army. Vehicle checks continue to be sent and are processed. Endless mugs of tea and coffee are consumed. Letters are written home, and before the night seems settled, dawn is breaking and another day begins. The first of July will no doubt be much like the thirtieth of June – such is the tragedy of Northern Ireland.

The Bomb-Disposal Men: A Day in the Life of an EOD Detachment

No branch of the British Army is more justly admired than the bomb-disposal men. Here we see what really goes on during one day in their lives.

It is 2215 hours, and the team room in a Detachment of 321 Explosive Ordnance Disposal Company is quiet except for the steady drone of the television in the corner and the occasional outburst from the Province Incident Radio Net (PIN). The team members are slumped in armchairs, watching a video of *Top Gun*. It's about the third or fourth time that they have seen it – the same is probably true for most of the videos on the camp. It is something to watch, however, and it makes the time go quickly when the team is not working. A cloud of cigarette smoke hangs over the group, slowly wafting over the television set and out through the open window. The non-smokers dislike the perpetual and pungent cloud, but have grown to accept it without serious complaint – it's the least of their worries.

The detachment is part of 321 Explosive Ordnance Disposal Company whose task, in Northern Ireland, of neutralising terrorist bombs (IEDs, or Improvised Explosive Devices, as they are officially known) has earned them worldwide respect. From humble beginnings, during the Malaya and Borneo campaigns, terrorist bomb disposal has become a sophisticated and deadly game played between these men and the terrorists. Some of their equipment is highly complex, some of it very simple. The training that they receive is comprehensive and the testing thorough. A high failure rate ensures that only those with the right aptitude for the job eventually make it to the Company. Their record is awe-inspiring. Since 1969 they have attended some 38,000 incidents and neutralised approximately 4,460 IEDs. In the course of this work eighteen operators have been killed. They are the most highly decorated unit in the British Army.

The Detachment Commander, a Captain and Ammunition Technical Officer (ATO) in the Royal Ordnance Corps, is busy writing up reports for the couple of incidents the team has attended during the preceding few days. He only glances up at the television occasionally, as he is intent on finishing these as quickly as possible in order to give himself time to write a letter home to his wife. In his late twenties, he finds himself having to conduct family business via telephone and letter. The two-month period between finishing his Special-to-Theatre EOD course at the School of Ammunition and arriving in the Province suddenly became two days' notice, due to a shortfall in EOD Operators. Consequently his wife has been left to fend for herself over a variety of matters. The

An Ammunition Technical Officer (ATO) donning his equipment on the site of a suspected Improvised Explosive Device (IED) – Army terminology for a terrorist bomb – so that he can make a close inspection of the device if necessary

same is true for many of the other Operators in the Company. Tonight on the phone she was sounding down; the washing machine had broken down and the cat was thought to have broken its hip. A trip to the vet had proved otherwise, but it was yet another worry on top of all the others. Wives with husbands in Northern Ireland worry, but in this job the worries are perhaps slightly greater. Terms like 'I'm fine' and 'there's no need to worry' don't cut much ice after two months away. Stresses are easily transmitted over the phone and fuel concern. Letters avoid this, which is why writing them becomes such an important part of the daily ritual.

Corporal M, or 'Bobo' to his colleagues, the team number two, is also only half watching the television. Having just finished updating the Ammunition Account for the previous week, he is busy filling in the end-of-month returns required by Company Headquarters. Training returns, ammo expenditure, equipment serial number, vehicle mileage – all have to be documented. Having only recently arrived in the Province, this is the first time he has had to do them, and they are taking him some time. Still, doing these rather than the outstanding equipment performance reports means that he doesn't have to use of the typewriter. The Captain seems to have got accustomed to single-finger typing but he, as yet, has not. Still, he's got five more months in which to practise.

Corporal L, the Royal Signals Operator, is half asleep in his chair. He thinks that he probably overdid it in the gym tonight. With only very limited recreational facilities available on the camp, the gym is popular. He promises himself an easier workout tomorrow.

The team escort, a soldier on loan from the Glosters, is making coffee. The job with the EOD team has been a real eye-opener for him. On previous tasks he has usually been on the cordon ringing the incident that the EOD team has been involved with, and cursing them for taking so long. Now he has had a chance to work with them and perhaps better understands the intricacies of their job.

The Captain stops writing and listens more intently to the speaker on the wall – the PIN net has got a lot busier all of a sudden. Then the message screams out – 'ATO request, possible mortar attack on RUC Cookstown, ICP Grid 483768.' The room suddenly becomes a hive of activity as the team spring into action. The escort races to the arms cabinet to withdraw the team's weapons, whilst the others run out to the garage to load the last of the equipment. Meanwhile the Captain is answering the phone. The local battalion have rung to give a few more details of the incident. Flak jackets and helmets are hastily pulled on as the team race out to their vehicles. A last-minute check by the Captain, and then the command 'Let's go!' is given and the vehicles move out. A flick of a switch and the flashing blue lights and two-tone horns shatter the relative peace of the night.

The barrier at the main gate is already open and the two vehicles shoot through and off into the darkness. The team drive at speed in the centre of the road, other vehicles permitting. Speed and distance from the road edge prob-

Wheelbarrow dealing with a suspect car bomb. The Wheelbarrow allows bomb disposal officers to deal with suspect bombs remotely. It has saved many lives

ably wouldn't make a lot of difference if a landmine was detonated as they went by, but doing it makes everyone feel better. Most of the vehicles they meet on the road move over to let them pass, but there are always the odd one or two who will be damned if they will. Tonight it is a Ford Escort with two male occupants. As the vans move right over to pass them one of the men gives the team the finger. It is ignored; however, he looks familiar and the vehicle registration number is mentally noted by the Captain, to be passed on when they have finished the task.

They quickly reach the incident scene. Troops have already cordoned off the surrounding area with white mine tape, which flutters in the slight breeze. Civilians, accompanied by RUC officers, can be seen moving away from the area, having just been evacuated from their houses. Two fire appliances, lights flashing, wait to one side, their hoses snaking away into the darkness where an explosion has broken all the street lighting. A figure is being carried into an ambulance. The two vans come to a halt in their standard configuration.

Corporal M and the escort start to off-load the equipment whilst the Captain speaks to the Incident Commander, an RUC Inspector, and the Cordon Commander, an Infantry Major. Apparently a lorry carrying a rubbish skip was hijacked in nearby Pomeroy several hours ago and the driver held at gunpoint. The terrorists then loaded a mortar launcher into the skip and drove the lorry into the council yard, just one hundred metres from the Police Station. The mortars were then fired, just as the evening shift was arriving. However, it would seem that only one launched successfully before an explosion occurred on the lorry itself. Several other mortar bombs have been thrown out into the darkness. None reached its intended target and the only casualties that the terrorists have caused are two passing civilians hit by flying glass and debris – one is seriously ill.

By the time the Captain returns, Corporal M has removed the 'Wheelbarrow' from the van, and is busy loading its weapons. This marvellous trackdriven robot is an essential part of the EOD team's equipment. Born out of a need to have some form of remote means to neutralise a device, it has been developed throughout the present campaign to its current form, the Mark 8. With its cameras, extending arms and weapons, it is a versatile machine, capable of disrupting a bomb without the Operator having to make a manual approach. On this job, however, it is only used to give a view of the smouldering remains of the skip and lorry.

A solid beam of light suddenly illuminates the scene as Nitesun, the heliborne lighting system, hovers overhead. With its aid, two unexploded mortar bombs are located. Both are embedded in the roof of a nearby school and so the Captain has to make a manual approach, without the benefit of wearing the EOD protective suit. He climbs up a ladder and on to the roof. In the flickering light he appears like a cat moving around cautiously. He is reminded of the Company emblem, Felix the cat, the helmeted feline with nine lives, and once again thinks how highly appropriate it is.

After some time the job is completed and the two mortar bombs have been neutralised. The long metal tubes, detonators, detonating cord and homemade explosives are laid out on the ground, whilst the Police and the host of other interested parties take photographs. The items are then bagged by the Scenes of Crime Officer, and a date is agreed with the Police for a statement to be taken. After debriefing the other agencies and packing their equipment, the EOD team leave and make their way back to base. The day is not yet over, however. All of the equipment has to be cleaned and prepared, ready to go again. The incident also has to be logged and the details passed over the phone for the Colonel's briefing at his daily conference later that morning. Corporal T, the REME technician, is dragged out of bed to repair a minor fault on the Wheelbarrow. His work usually starts when the team return from a task. It is 0320 before the team finally get to bed, with the Captain promising them a lie-in until 1000 hours.

The telephone rings at exactly 0930. It is the local Battalion Ops Room. A patrol in the city centre was crossing a road when a small explosion occurred near a fence-post. There have been no casualties but ATO is once again required to clear the scene. This time it is only a five-minute journey through the narrow streets. However, the route takes them over a culvert near the hospital. An IED was once placed there before, and the team never like driving over it. A little extra speed and crossed fingers is normal – this time is no exception.

Soon the Wheelbarrow is trundling down the road towards the explosion site, and it is established that an IED positioned in a hole by the fence-post and fired through a wire appears to have only partially exploded. The main charge

Wheelbarrow needs regular maintenance. Here it is being checked over back in base after an operation

The EOD team preparing Wheelbarrow on the site of an Improvised Explosive Device (IED). Note the operator's colleague providing cover against outside interference

is still in the hole. Wheelbarrow attempts to pull the bag from the hole, but it is too heavy. Once again the Captain will have to make a manual approach. He stands, arms outstretched like an ancient knight, whilst the remainder of the team dress him in the EOD suit.

Weighing some 60 lb, the suit is designed to give limited protection against flying fragments. If a large IED exploded near him, however, it would do little except keep him reasonably in one piece. On cold days it does have the advantage of keeping him warm, but on hot days it can be unbearably uncomfortable. On a recent job, neutralising an 800-lb landmine, he lost nearly half a stone whilst wearing the suit. Nevertheless, it is a psychological comfort. With his portable equipment – weapon, tool bag and hook and line – the weight, as he shuffles out of the ICP, is up to about 70 lb. It is a long lonely walk down to where the Wheelbarrow now sits, forlornly peering at the fence-post. The Captain looks constantly from side to side, ready to react to anything suspicious. By the time he reaches the post he is sweating profusely. The dis-

Part of a 5 UDR cordon around a bomb on the railway link between Northern Ireland and Eire. The IRA regularly attempt to disrupt this line as part of their campaign of economic warfare against the state

Soldiers from 6 UDR prepare to fly out from their base in a Lynx helicopter. Helicopters are used to mount operations such as snap roadblocks or to deposit surveillance teams in rural areas

tinctive smell of diesel and marzipan, the smell of terrorist home-made explosive, is obvious even from ten metres away. The bag is difficult to get a hold on, but eventually he manages to secure a line to it and troops back up the road to the waiting vehicles. As soon as he is back his team are around him, removing the protective plates and helmet in order to ease the discomfort for a while.

A pull on the line, and the bag is out of the hole, its contents spilled out into the road. The task is soon completed after this, and the team are pleased to hear that a local IRA member has been arrested in connection with the incident. Neutralising IEDs is one thing, but actually getting a terrorist into court and hopefully prison is the main aim. It's a cheering bonus when this happens.

Upon return to their base the Captain disappears to the Ops Room to brief them about the incident, whilst his team once again prepare the equipment. Once that is completed the Captain is joined by Corporal L for a planning conference on a forthcoming job of clearing some derelict houses of a suspect IED. It was not scheduled until later that night, but since the ATO team are there they decide to get it out of the way. The team don't complain as it means an extra journey and a possible late night being avoided.

By 1800 hours the team are back home, watching the television. In their self-contained kitchen the microwave is busy heating up their evening meal. They could eat in the main cookhouse, but tonight they prefer their own culinary efforts. The Captain is in his office, once again completing the daily incident log and contemplating more reports that have to be written. He's in the middle of a correspondence promotion course and the books line his desk. He thought he would have plenty of time to study. Things, however, have turned out slightly differently and the books have remained largely unopened.

Suddenly the phone rings: a suspect car bomb in the city centre. Once again the room becomes a hive of activity, and the evening meal is forgotten. They wait, kitted up and vehicles running, for ten minutes before the phone rings again and they are told to stand down; it was a false alarm. A sigh of relief. The vehicles are put away again, and the now cold and slightly unappetising evening meal is pushed back into the microwave.

It is 2130 and the EOD team are grouped around the television set again, cigarette smoke spiralling up to the ceiling. The Captain is reading the paper, Corporal L is making the coffee and Corporal M is half asleep. Everyone is contemplating an early night – it has been a long day, one of the busiest for a while. All is quiet. The radio suddenly chatters into life; the phone rings. . . .

The Ulster Defence Regiment

The Ulster Defence Regiment live with the Northern Ireland problem every day of their lives. This chapter tells us what it's like.

As dawn broke on 30 June the lines of white tape became more obvious to the two soldiers lying in the ditch, a little way up the road. A flashing amber light reflected off the red and white signboards, which simply read 'Road Closed'. The scene was all too familiar to the soldiers, both from C Company of the 5th (County Londonderry) Battalion of the Ulster Defence Regiment, but on this occasion the circumstances were rather unusual. At 0700 hours the previous morning a bomb had exploded under the engine of a passenger train, just before an unmanned level crossing on the main Belfast to Londonderry railway line, in the north-west of Northern Ireland. 5 UDR, in whose district the incident took place, immediately became responsible for cordoning the area in order to create a safe space within which the specialists from the Royal Army Ordnance Corps, Royal Engineers and Royal Ulster Constabulary could work, examining and collecting forensic evidence, as well as ensuring that the remainder of the line was clear of any further devices. The cordon, supported by joint mobile patrols from the RUC and other elements of the battalion, remained in place until the whole area was declared clear at 1600 hours on 30 June, and responsibility for operations in the area was handed back to the police. C Company withdrew to barracks in order to rest before embarking on the next operation early the following morning.

As the vehicle convoy turned through the barrack gates, so too did the first of the battalion's part-timers, arriving to begin their duty. Many of the part-timers report for duty for twelve nights every month. They leave their civilian jobs, and instead of heading for home and a quiet night in front of the television, report in to their company bases, change into military uniform and are briefed for the night's patrol tasks, which will take them through until the early hours of the morning, when they again become civilians. The part-time element of a battalion is made up from all sections of the community: farmers, solicitors, factory workers, office managers, garage mechanics and the unemployed, to name but a few, all united by the common desire to see their country rid of terrorism. A large number of the part-timers have been reporting for duty for the entire twenty years of the Ulster Defence Regiment's existence.

Fifty miles south-west of the railway line bomb, 13 Platoon of 6 UDR reported in for duty at 0600; they had been hoping for a quiet day, in order to catch up on some training. However, three days earlier an RUC reserve constable had been murdered by the IRA using an under-vehicle booby trap. 13 Platoon had subsequently been tasked with providing the security for the funeral, which was to be held in a small village near Strabane. The operation had been planned the previous day after close liaison with the local RUC Headquarters, and was to include a detailed search of the area using dogs and helicopters. The platoon was ready for briefing by 0700, and by 0830 they were in position on the ground, having been flown from their barracks in Omagh some twenty miles away. Once in position, the platoon began to search the funeral route, as well as the churchyard and cemetery. It was here that the dogs came into their own, casting about for any tell-tale scent that would betray the presence of a hidden bomb. The soldiers meanwhile were looking into back gardens, dustbins and under hedgerows. The search lasted until 1130 hours, after which the platoon took up positions along the route and established vehicle checkpoints on roads throughout the area. These were moved frequently so that terrorists could never be sure where the next checkpoint would be. As the time for the funeral approached, so the RUC began to arrive to take over on point duty from the UDR, who then merged into the background but nevertheless maintained a discreet but ever-watchful presence.

The funeral passed off without incident, and by 1630 hours the majority of the platoon was able to return to Omagh, leaving a section under the command of the platoon commander to cover the post-funeral gathering in the church hall. The cordon was eventually lifted at 1900 hours and the section flown home, only to prepare for a very full day's patrolling on the following day. The day's missed training would have to be fitted in some other time.

In Belfast, the day started on a humorous note when, at 0130 hours, the top cover sentry of a mobile patrol from one of the companies of 7th/10th (City of Belfast) Battalion noticed that the front door of a bank was wide open. The patrol dismounted from their vehicles and, having informed the battalion operations room of their find, deployed around the bank to await the arrival of the RUC. As the patrol commander approached the door of the bank, he spotted a black briefcase leaning against a wall. He immediately withdrew the patrol to a safe distance and together they began to clear the area for any other suspicious signs. The street was soon cleared and an incident control point was set up. The RUC arrived, a sergeant in command. The patrol commander had just finished briefing the police on the situation when one of the patrol shouted, 'There's someone in the bank.' The patrol gave cover as the police approached the building. Just at that moment a man staggered out of the door of the bank; when he saw the tableau of police and soldiers in front of him, he threw his arms up in the air. The RUC sergeant went forward and arrested the man, who turned out to be the bank security guard who was rather the worse for drink, and had forgotten to lock the door! The whole incident was over within an hour and the patrol was able to return to their base.

South-east of Belfast lies rural County Down, the tactical area of responsibility of 3 UDR. D Company had spent the previous day digging a line of trenches to cover a series of vehicle checkpoints on all the main roads, and were just settling down for their first day's occupation of the trenches. For a change the weather was fine, and when shortly after midnight the company second in command went round to visit the soldiers in the trenches, he found morale

Top cover sentries on a 7/10 UDR mobile patrol

high. One of the new breed of Sandhurst-trained officers in the regiment, he has also attended the Platoon Commanders' Battle Course at the School of Infantry, and is well versed in the principles of living in a defensive position. When he had finished visiting all the positions he returned to his base at Ballykinler in time to get a couple of hours' sleep before briefing the helicopter pilots who were to fly in support of the checkpoint operation.

The helicopters lifted off at 1030 hours. Having criss-crossed the ground, the aerial spotter sighted a van being driven suspiciously, near one of the dug-in positions. The pilot dipped the nose of the aircraft and dropped down behind the van, close enough to be able to read its registration number: only a delivery van from the nearby town.

The static checkpoint operation continued for most of the day, relieved only

115

when elements of the company were flown from their entrenched positions to set up snap checkpoints on roads that could not be covered permanently. By early evening the company second in command had exchanged his helicopter for a Land-Rover, and was out visiting the platoons in their trenches again, before returning to barracks to brief the part-time soldiers who were taking over the mobile patrolling tasks for the night. The briefing over, he returned to the countryside to join his company commander in his trench to see out the remainder of the night.

Not every battalion had such a busy day. In East Tyrone, 8 UDR started the day on a happy note when the Commanding Officer called the Administrative Officer to his office and told him that he was to be promoted to Captain. This was followed by the Company Commander of B Company being asked to organise a barbecue around the swimming pool (the legacy of a former Commanding Officer who had discovered an under-used JCB in the grounds of the base). In the Operations Room, some of the female part-time watchkeepers were just coming on duty and were being briefed on the operations that were planned for the day and those that were already taking place. The UDR has some 700 women in its ranks; they are fully integrated into the regiment and, although they do not carry weapons, perform the same duties as their male counterparts.

The air operations officer was in the middle of co-ordinating the helicopter tasking for the day, when a Wessex landed beside the swimming pool, causing part of the screen fencing to blow into the pool and OC B Company to have a minor sense of humour failure. In Battalion Headquarters, the Welfare Officer was busy co-ordinating holidays for the children of soldiers who have been killed by terrorists, when a call was received to say that the grave of a terrorist victim had been vandalised. Forgetting the holidays temporarily, she headed out in her car to assess the damage for herself. Thankfully, the damage was minimal and she was able to return to barracks knowing that the Battalion Welfare Fund would be able to pay for the cost of the necessary repairs. Later in the day she was busy again when the Intelligence Officer informed her that it had become necessary for a UDR soldier and his family to move from their present house. The well-tested welfare organisation swung into gear, as the Welfare Officer once again climbed into her car to go and speak to the wife and assure her that temporary accommodation had been arranged for her and the family, and that the move from one house to another would be made as smooth as possible. As the Welfare Officer drove back through the camp gates she was greeted by the smell of a well-smouldering barbecue and the news that the Greenfinch rounders team had lost heavily in a tournament at RAF Aldergrove. It hadn't been an unusual day.

Although 1/9 UDR in Antrim and 11 UDR in Portadown passed relatively uneventful days in their respective areas, another day it might have been their turn to face the sort of challenges met by 3, 5, 6, 7/10 and 8 UDR on 30 June 1989. These brave men and women face the threat of terrorism every day of the year.

* * *

My name is Private A and I am a part-time soldier in the 4th (County Fermanagh) Battalion of the Ulster Defence Regiment. Each week I try to do at least three duties, and Friday 30 June was my third that week. It had been a long hot day on the farm where I help my father with his large dairy herd. As it is the hay and silage season, we had been going non-stop since dawn. My mother had a big spread waiting for us that evening when we got cleared up, and then it was time to report to the UDR base for patrol duty. I got my personal weapon and kit together, checked under the car, and headed for Angelo. The lads were already at the armoury drawing their rifles, then there was the briefing. We were due to go out at 2000 hours. Great, a change from mobiles: it was a boat patrol and rummage search of an island close to the border, where there is a constant high threat of attack from a cross-border shoot. A great night for it, and those Rigid Raiders are the fastest boats on the Lough. We left Angelo by Land-Rover with the boats in tow, and put them in the water

A UDR boat patrol passes Enniskillen Castle. In Ulster there are several large inland lakes or sea loughs. This is the most efficient way of covering these areas

at a nearby jetty. No time wasted, away within seconds at top speed. It gave the cabin cruiser set a thrill to see us in action. You wouldn't think there was a war on, the way the tourists can't stay away, but who can blame them in weather like this? Wouldn't have minded sipping pink gins aboard a cruiser myself, but the job's got to be done and we have got plenty worth fighting for.

A speedy journey in the boats took us to one of the 365 islands in Lough Erne. We carry out rummage searches of the islands to deter such activities as smuggling, and terrorists from using them as locations for weapon hides.

Within minutes of disembarking from the boats and starting the search we all found to our disappointment that the good weather still hadn't dried out the long grass of the islands, and we were all soon soaking. The search was completed at dusk. The boats picked us up at a pre-arranged rendezvous and we sped off again to do a foot patrol on the lough shore road. As it was Friday night, nearing the end of our tour of duty, there was plenty of traffic on the road as people came home from pubs and dances. As our pick-up time approached we mustered under our patrol commander and soon moved back to base, tired but satisfied that we'd done a good job.

After the patrol debrief, I changed, collected my personal weapon and returned home. With any luck my father wouldn't call me for the milking too early; he generally doesn't when I've been out on patrol the night before. Getting in after half past three to get up again at six o'clock is no fun. At least on the farm I can work 'flexi-time', not like some of the boys who have to be at their civvy job at half eight in the morning. As I approached the house, I noticed that my parents' bedroom light was still on. It always is on the nights I'm out with the UDR. They pretend for my sake they don't worry. I turned the key in the door and crept in. As I climbed the stairs my Dad's voice called out with relief as he always does, 'Is that yourself, son?'

Europe

Swords into Ploughshares: The UN Battalion in Cyprus

Captain P Watkins

The British Army has provided troops for the UN all over the world. Here Captain Phillip Watkins, holding the appointment of Humanitarian Officer with the Royal Horse Artillery, describes a day in his life in Cyprus whilst wearing the blue beret of the UN.

'And then sixty sit-ups, stand by, go.' It's 0700 on 30 June and my body has already been up for an hour and run four miles. The rest of me is just catching up. The PT instructor barks out his orders with an enthusiasm that is unnatural for this time of the morning. Members of Headquarters Battery follow them with varying degrees of success. In the case of the postal orderly, his sixty sit-ups must be on a cumulative basis. We have been here five months and he has one month left to complete his sixty. By contrast the Sergeant Major has already finished, and is jogging on the spot with an air of contempt for the rest of us mere mortals.

My mind has at last caught up, and indeed overtaken my body. It's ahead in the shower, imagining the delight of hot water. In the event, the water is far from hot – the EOKA gunmen who were once interned in this camp probably relied on the same boiler for water, and I am sure it was with a wry sense of humour that the Greek Cypriot government allocated St David's Camp to the British contingent of the UN Forces in Cyprus.

After a quick breakfast it's across to HQ to read the sitreps (situation reports). Each of the two sub-units of the British contingent manning the BZ (Buffer Zone) has sent in a sitrep detailing the previous twenty-four hours' activity in the BZ. A quick scan to see if anything has happened in my department. As the Sector Humanitarian Officer, one of my concerns is farming activity within the Buffer Zone.

I see from the sitreps that a farmer has been escorted out of the BZ by the UN soldiers from the western sub-unit, for farming in an unauthorised area. Today it's a Greek Cypriot farmer who is cultivating land too close to the Turkish military positions for the UN to guarantee his safety. It is just as likely to have been a Turkish Cypriot farmer moving too far south. Allowing farming in the BZ is the best means available to the UN to achieve its stated aim of contributing to the restoration of normal conditions. It is also the point at which the divided communities meet, and if the expansion is to continue without incident it must be closely regulated. Passes are issued and soldiers act as escorts to any farmer who may feel insecure.

120

Captain Watkins discusses the finer points of farming with a local

Many of the tasks of soldiers of the UN battalion are of this humanitarian nature, rather than purely operational. Later today, soldiers from the eastern sub-unit, which is located on the outskirts of Nicosia, will provide an escort for an Armenian funeral. The cemetery is situated inside the BZ only 200 metres from the Turkish military positions: the presence of UN blue berets will reassure both sides.

By 0815 we are half-way through the Commanding Officer's morning conference. Each department head is responsible for briefing the Colonel. The Operations Officer has briefed us on a shot fired from one of the Turkish observation towers. The situation is that the UN Commander of the area requested information on the shot from the Turkish forces. They reported it as a negligent discharge during a change of the guard. The matter is now closed; the explanation is plausible, it happens with alarming frequency on both sides. I have reported on the illegal farming to the CO, and now it's the turn of the Operations Information Officer. I think it's fair to say that the only significant report from the Operations Information Officer during this tour has been the

A beach landing in Cyprus adds realism to military training

dates of the first flights bringing Swedish holidaymakers to Larnaca. Today's information on the movement of a Greek Cypriot National Guard convoy pales into insignificance.

The Colonel runs through his diary for the day. He has a meeting with Colonel Charalambedes, the Officer in Command of National Guard forces in our area. Following this the Colonel is to visit Dhekelia, where the two other sub-units which form the other half of the battalion are providing security for the British Garrison.

Regular visits by the Colonel and the Adjutant ensure that the HQ element, which remains in the Buffer Zone for six months, does not lose touch with the two sub-units, which rotate to these duties after three months with the UN. The Colonel will first visit the sub-unit guarding the Signals Regiment based at Ayios Nikolaos, and then go on to the sub-unit at Dhekelia. Both sub-units are involved in internal security duties which demand long hours of vigilance, which must be managed carefully to avoid routine and monotony.

To help provide variety for the UN battalion, as well as refresher training, troops of twenty-six soldiers will embark on two weeks of Adventurous and Military Training. Today the Adjutant is visiting troops who are mounting a heliborne assault on the village of Paramali, as a culmination of their week of military training. (The Operations Information Officer tells me the Adjutant is really going to Dhekelia to water-ski – but then Operations Information is seldom accurate!)

122

After a run through the Adjutant's forecast of events, revealing yet two more VIPs visiting the battalion later in the month, the morning prayers change tack. The Regimental Sergeant Major, responsible for co-ordinating sporting activity in addition to his normal duty, reports that a number of soldiers from the regiment are going on a sailing course. Opportunities for water sports are good on the island, and the RSM is able to get most of the soldiers on one short course, such as canoeing or diving, during the tour.

The daily conference over, it's on to the main activity of the day for me, which is a Long Northwind Patrol. Outside the UNBZ, the Humanitarian Officer has responsibilities for visiting the enclaved people of this divided island; that is Greek Cypriots still living in the North, and Turkish Cypriots still living in the South. Each of these communities receives visits from the UN, and today we are going to the North.

In the British contingent's area of responsibility there is the town of Kyrenia, and the Maronite villages of Asomatos, Karpasha and Kormakiti, which nestle in the western foothills of the Kyrenia mountain range. The Maronites are Greek-speaking Catholics living in Turkish-held territory, and as if that were not enough of a mixture, in order to maintain links with their Lebanese roots they hold their church services in Arabic.

Today I will lead a convoy of UN lorries with food and gas to these villages. The aim of the patrols is couched in high ideals of maintaining peace, aiding the world food programme and supporting the International Red Cross. At a practical level, we see fair play, and deliver the groceries.

The rest of the Humanitarian team, Staff Sergeant Punter, Sergeant McMenemy and Sergeant Rylance left camp early this morning (missing the sixty sit-ups!) to supervise the loading of the lorries. They will rendezvous with me at the Turkish Checkpoint in Nicosia. My first visit is to the Red Cross, to pick up medicines requested on the previous patrol and then on to visit the Franciscan nuns, who run a school in Nicosia. We visit the Sisters for two reasons. The first is that that three nuns from the same order work in the largest of the villages, Kormakiti, and so we provide a useful link. The second reason is that they always give us a packed lunch!

At the Turkish Checkpoint, paperwork complete, we meet up with Sergeant Nafi, a legend of the Levant. Sergeant Nafi is a Turkish Cypriot policeman who has accompanied these patrols for the last fourteen years. He knows all the villagers personally, and is as indispensible to me as he was to the previous twenty-seven Humanitarian Officers.

Before midday we arrive at the first village and are met by the Mukhtar, Hadji Hanna. The Mukhtar is the elected head of the village, and all requests or problems are passed through him to me. The average age of the villagers is over seventy, and in this village, Asomatos, there are only twenty-seven Maronites left. These are dying communities whose youth has moved to the prosperous South; requests are therefore those associated with old age.

As the lorries are unloaded I am aware of a disturbance. Sergeant Nafi gives me a knowing look and I realise we are about to see a repeat performance of the Greek tragedy play. It's a play I have seen acted regularly in each village, and on every occasion it's exactly the same. The goods delivered consist of everyday groceries, and they are busily collected by the villagers and thrust into bags. It's not the first delivery of food after a famine, but the scene suggests it could be. Suddenly, but predictably, the main actor enters the stage and speaks in a piercing voice, intelligible to me only because it is unmistakably one of alarm. With true Mediterranean emotion the hands move to the face to emphasise tragedy. The finger is then pointed. The second actor, the accused, immediately begins a soliloquy of defence. Soon they are joined by the supporting cast taking sides. The language difference is unimportant, the plot is clear. Something is missing, and somebody is clearly guilty – 'whodunnit?'

Sergeant Nafi looks at me, sighs and closes his eyes. I know it's time for audience participation. He rises slowly, but then delivers a fierce tirade of which any Sergeant Major would be proud. The villagers are stunned into silence and turn to face me, centre stage now, but I do not have a speaking part. Instead I put on my best British Empire District Commissioner look of authority while Sergeant Nafi begins to search. He proves the accused innocent, and then, surprise, surprise, we find the missing item, Halloumi cheese, in the bottom of one of the delivery boxes. The tragedy turns into comedy. We all share the joke and then the lemon squash!

After an uneventful visit to the thirty-seven villagers of Karpasha, we arrive in the village of Kormakiti, which has 215 residents. Not all today's requests are routine. Sister Agnesey enquires if any progress has been made in acquiring commodes. The request was first submitted a number of months ago, but all attempts through the usual channels have failed. The sisters are concerned and making an impassioned plea. They invite me to visit one of the needy. We step off the main road, down two steps and into one of two rooms which constitute home. There is no electric light, and the floor is compacted earth. A picture of the Virgin Mary and a cross are the only wall decorations, and the furniture consists of a single chair and a table. In the corner of the room is a large bed hung with a dark musty surrounding curtain. The smell is human, raw, and overpowering. I am greeted by a timid and frail old man who, clutching his hands nervously, thanks me for coming: a greeting he continues to offer throughout my stay. Sister Agnesey leads me to the bed on which lies Maria Frantzia, the old man's wife; she smiles and we exchange a few words. Maria has lived paralysed in this bed for thirty years. The experience is sobering, a renewed effort has to be made to obtain commodes.

Writing the patrol report back in St David's Camp, I am able to state that the four ladies in Kyrenia are all well. With the paperwork finished, it's across to the Mess for a cup of tea and to catch up on the rest of the news.

The last task of the day for the humanitarian branch is to visit the village of Mammari and speak to the local farmers. The meetings are usually relaxed and informal, and tonight is no exception. Turkish coffees are brought to the table, together with vegetables soaked in lemon juice. The farmers from this village own land in the Buffer Zone that has been lying fallow for fourteen years, but which is now being opened up. When we began the project we were inundated with farmers waving *korchanis* (land title deeds) to the relevant fields. Five months into the project, we are now at a manageable level and tonight we arrange to open a further six fields over the next week.

Decorating the walls of this particular coffee shop are pictures of EOKA gunmen, reminders of past struggles. Today, thankfully, the acrimony is forgotten and only the coffee is bitter. The meeting is over within an hour and we return to the camp.

Walking from the Regimental Headquarters to the Mess there is time to reflect on the day and think about the future. My day is over, but the soldiers on the line will continue to man observation posts and patrol throughout the night. In four weeks' time the regiment moves from peacekeeping with the United Nations to peacekeeping by deterrent in West Germany. My thoughts are then interrupted by a tired and strained voice: '. . . forty-eight, forty-nine, fifty. . . .' It's 2030 hours and the postal orderly struggles on.

Ed. note: Two weeks later the first commode was delivered to Maria Frantzia.

A British-manned UN checkpoint in Cyprus

ACE Mobile Force Supply Company: Royal Army Ordnance Corps

The Allied Command Europe Mobile Force is a NATO organisation. One of Britain's contributions is the provision of the bulk of the manpower for the supply company.

It is five o'clock in the morning, but already the sun has crept over the horizon and the temperature is rising. Ten days ago the AMF(L) Supply Company RAOC arrived in northern Turkey to support the multinational Allied Command Europe Mobile Force (Land), (AMF(L)), as part of the Logistic Support Battalion. The climate, terrain and culture of the region could not be more different from that which they had experienced in northern Norway only three months earlier. The temperature in Bardufoss regularly reached minus 30°C; here on the outskirts of Corlu it is frequently plus 35°C at midday. Physical fitness is most important for coping with these extremes of climate, because lengthy periods of acclimatisation are not possible – work must start immediately on arrival in a new theatre of operations.

The company base moved from its deterrent operations location two days ago. Gone now are all the flags and signs of welcome to the world's press and senior military guests. The Force welcomes visitors, because its primary role is deterrent, and the Force can best fulfil its mission by showing how effectively a multinational, integrated force can operate in isolated locations on the flanks of Europe. The company's location is a wide area of open, rolling countryside, parched grassland dissected by open dry fissures. Finely woven desert camouflage nets cover all our tents and equipment, blending well with the terrain. Despite the total lack of natural foliage, or local buildings, the company is well hidden from ground and aerial observation. Fortunately the AMF(L) Supply Company has its own mobile shower unit co-located with it, and this is a very popular port of call first thing in the morning and throughout the evening.

The Company Command Post is already a hive of activity as the daily reports are being collated on a computer, ready for transmission to Battalion Headquarters. A member of the Stores Platoon is engrossed with the fax machine in another corner of the tent, passing demands for urgently required spare parts, not available in theatre, to the Logistic Operations Centre at SHAPE (Supreme Headquarters Allied Powers in Europe) at Mons in Belgium. A member of the German Wire Company is conducting a line test on one of the telephones, and the Turkish interpreter, a young, olive-skinned Lance-Corporal with only two of his eighteen months' national service remaining, and known to all by his first name of Ercan because his surname is unpronounceable in English, is standing near the entrance drinking coffee and smoking a foul-smelling cigarette.

126

Captain Piervittorio Stefanoni, the Italian Force Veterinary Officer, arrives at the entrance to the Command Post. He is a small, bearded, rather rotund man in his late thirties, always jovial and yet a true professional who takes his responsibilities very seriously. Accompanied by Major Clive Elderton, the Company Commander, and the interpreter, they set off for the local slaughterhouse some ten kilometres away. They pass a pair of very solemn Turkish sentries from the Host Nation Support Unit, receiving a rather lethargic response to their cheery wave. A brief halt at the Military Police Post to book out with the Belgian Military Policeman on duty, and they are off along the main road into Corlu. Despite the early hour – it is not yet 0600 hours – the road is busy with overcrowded buses, ancient taxis and slow-moving, overloaded cargo vehicles. This is the main highway from Istanbul, which lies about 100 miles to the east, to the Greek border, some 100 miles to the west, and although in most parts it has a good tarmac surface it is in the main single carriageway. The locals go to suicidal lengths to overtake vehicles travelling only marginally slower than themselves.

Entering Corlu it is apparent that the street traders have already reserved their pitches, and a queue has formed outside the baker's shop. Ragged children wearing a semblance of black and white uniform skip along the pavements on their way to school; by midday their schooling will be over for the day and they will start work alongside their parents, or engage in various enterprises from shoe shining to the selling of postcards. Other children, destined for the afternoon session in the schoolhouse, are already at work. Outside the local military headquarters the Turkish Military Police stand guard. They have Kalashnikov rifles slung ready across their chests and wear distinctive red and white armbands and helmets. These are the *Asiz*, and are a common sight throughout the Turkish military.

The slaughterhouse is on the outskirts of the town, and can be smelled before it comes into view. The NATO party arrive to find the local butcher has already assembled a dozen healthy-looking beasts behind the main building ready for inspection. Captain Stefanoni sets to work immediately, examining flanks, ears and tongues, and soon selects the five beasts required to feed five thousand multinational customers. The Turkish slaughtermen offer the ubiquitous Turkish tea, a strong bitter brew known as *chi*, which invariably precedes all conversations, and the RAOC Master Butcher and his three British and two Belgian butchers, who have been busy all night cutting and jointing, now prepare themselves to assist in the slaughter of the cattle and sheep. The Muslim religion dictates that this is a particularly bloody affair, but the special skills of these tradesmen have, in a very short period, led to mutual respect and friendship, despite a total language barrier.

The next port of call is back in the town, where other members of the Ration Platoon will be busy collecting the day's fresh fruit and vegetable order. The driver pulls up outside a small, somewhat dilapidated shop in the back streets. A Turkish two-and-a-half-ton truck from the Host Nation Support Unit is parked outside, and several members of the Company, assisted by an Italian and a German soldier, are busy loading the truck with all manner of fresh produce. In the door of the shop stands the owner, with the Company's Ration

Warrant Officer conducting individual qualitative and quantitative checks on what is being loaded on to the vehicle. A break is taken, instantly *chi* appears and the visitors are presented with an enormous banana, a great delicacy in this region. Pleasantries are exchanged; seemingly all is well; however, the quality of oranges is rather poor today, and nectarines will have to be issued in lieu! Elsewhere in the town other RAOC victuallers from the Ration Platoon are collecting the order for dry goods and dairy products. The next port of call, however, is the Petroleum Platoon, who are operating a Bulk Fuel Installation adjacent to the main road leading to Istanbul.

The platoon have constructed the fuel farm and are currently receiving a bulk inload from PetroFisi, the main Turkish fuel supplier. The large rubber pillow tanks lie on rubber sheeting within earth walls, dug to the Platoon Commander's specification by a local contractor. A wide assortment of fuel tankers is parked in the area: German and British Unit Bulk Refuellers, enormous American tankers, an Italian kerosene tanker and two distinctive red and white PetroFisi tankers. Soldiers from all eight NATO nations participating in the exercise are hard at work operating pumping equipment, dispensing fuel to unit refuellers, receiving fuel from the PetroFisi tankers into the pillow tanks, and refuelling an assortment of military vehicles from a kerbside facility. Nearby a specially-trained RAOC Petroleum Operator is testing the specification of the fuel being delivered. His portable laboratory is set up in a small tent which is unbearably hot, and could well do without the added heat from his bunsen burner. Meanwhile other members of the platoon work under the watchful eye of the Royal Engineer Petroleum Fitter Corporal, who is struggling to keep the fuel pumps running despite the dust and searing heat.

A message arrives at the Platoon Command Post requesting fire-fighting assistance; it transpires that a Turkish vehicle carrying British ammunition has overturned and that fuel is leaking from the ruptured fuel tank. The Platoon Sergeant loads the necessary extinguishers and fire-fighting equipment into the back of a vehicle and they speed off.

The accident has occurred a few hundred metres from the Turkish depot in which ammunition is stored for the Force. The Sergeant Ammunition Technician RAOC working in the depot was first on the scene, and managed to evacuate the driver and passenger of the vehicle by German Huey helicopter to the AMF(L) Italian Field Hospital. It transpired later that neither was seriously injured. The *Asiz* were already at the scene of the accident, and the arrival of the company's interpreter did much to help communication between the *Asiz*, the local fire brigade and the British Sergeant. He managed to move most of the ammunition away from the fuel but some would only be accessible when the vehicle was righted by the recovery section from the AMF(L) Workshop. With the situation well under control it is time to return to the Company HQ.

Over a lunch of cold meat salad, bread from the RAOC mobile field bakery and fresh fruit, in the communal dining tent the Company Commander hears how a member of the Stores Platoon spent most of the morning trying to purchase Bedford truck spares. The Turks are particularly skilled at copying all manner of goods, and the young RAOC Supply Specialist Corporal visited six

Bedford suppliers in the local town, and drank at least a gallon of *chi*, before he was satisfied that he was buying genuine Bedford parts! Meal times provide a marvellous forum for stories, some wildly exaggerated, others somewhat embarrassing. It seems that another Lance-Corporal from the Stores Platoon, responsible for running the Force laundry contract, somehow managed to get all his personal laundry starched and pressed. The perk backfired, however, for when he collected his bundle it was so heavily starched he could not break into either his trouser legs or jacket sleeves! Language, it would seem, is no barrier to soldiers' stories, for when this little gem emerged the Italians, Belgians and Germans in the dining tent erupted in fits of laughter along with their British workmates.

Napoleon is meant to have said that an army marches on its stomach. Bread forms the basis of the daily diet and the AMF makes its own

A post-lunch cup of coffee in the Command Post is interrupted by an air-raid warning and an increase in the threat of chemical attack. After one hour in NBC (nuclear, bacteriological and chemical) protective clothing and respirator, life gets extremely uncomfortable. The NBC suit is definitely not designed for wear in hot climates; the outcome of this episode is an attack by Belgian F-16s, which results in several simulated casualties. These events hamper the breakdown and issue of fresh and combat rations to the Force, and the Bath Unit is prepared in case it is necessary to deal with decontamination. Clearance patrols are mounted to ensure that our area is clear of the enemy.

After dinner it is time to visit the bakers, hard at work in the mobile field bakery. The heat inside the oven and preparation containers is almost unbearable, and yet the bakers survive shifts of twelve hours at a time. In Norway in winter the smell of freshly baked bread, and the warmth from the containers, are great attractions, and visitors seem to congregate around the bakery like bees around a honey pot. Not so in Turkey, where bakers can lose several pounds in weight during each shift. As night comes the temperature drops slightly, bringing a little respite.

Another day over, typical of many others for the AMF(L) Supply Company RAOC on exercise in support of the multinational Force. Time to reflect that the next deployment is to Denmark in the autumn, then Norway in winter, before the delights of northern Italy in spring. However, there are a further two weeks in Turkey yet, time to visit the Blue Mosque in Istanbul, haggle for genuine Turkish carpets in the Grand Bazaar and take part in what promises to be an emotional but fascinating tour of the Gallipoli Battlefields.

The Royal Army Medical Corps: A Day in the Life of 3 Armoured Field Ambulance BAOR

Men as well as equipment have to 'repaired' in battle. This is the task of the men of the Royal Army Medical Corps. Here we see them training for that role.

There was a hollow empty echo as the Quartermaster slammed the door of the 3rd Armoured Field Ambulance regimental headquarters. Almost everybody was away. He went out of the gate, wondering what the rest of the unit had been doing. It was just another day in the life of 3rd Armoured Field Ambulance. A Squadron were on a training exercise in Vogelsang, B Squadron were providing the medical support to the Nijmegen Marches in Holland, and Private Johnson was on an individual medical attachment to BATUS (the British Army Training Unit Suffield) in Canada.

The Vogelsang Training Centre is an impressive facility. Formerly it was a prestige camp designed for the cream of the Hitler Youth. In those days Vogelsang was a type of Butlins for Brownshirts. Nowadays it is maintained as a NATO Training Centre.

Literally translated, *Vogelsang* means 'bird song', but it was some time before the dawn chorus when the Squadron Sergeant Major bawled out the orders for reveille. As a young private reluctantly eased himself out of his sleeping bag, he was heard to say, 'I thought there was only one 5.30 in the day, and that is after tea.'

At 0600 hours, A Squadron was on parade in PT kit. Some individuals looked far from the Army image of the lean, mean fighting machine. Even so, an exciting timed race around the challenging assault course on the hill produced some impressive performances. This invigorating start to the day ended with a cold shower, and by 0730 a substantial breakfast had been polished off. The appetite of the British soldier is enormous, neither a rasher of bacon nor a crumb of bread was left to feed the birds.

A Squadron had been divided into sections for the first period of their military training. Privates scampered around trying to locate missing items of personal kit, NCOs were supervising the application of camouflage cream on the faces of section personnel, and squadron officers were discussing the final plans for the training.

Basic infantry tactics were taught by guest instructors invited to join the Squadron from the Royal Scots (The Royal Regiment), the Royal Regiment of Fusiliers, and the Queen's Lancashire Regiment. By the end of the first lesson some medics seemed so confused that they could not explain the difference between an arrowhead formation and a reef knot.

Urban combat creates particularly difficult conditions for the removal of a casualty. Here 20 Field Ambulance practise their technique at Vogelsang

Everyone seems to enjoy loud bangs, so during a lesson on trip flares attention was riveted on the NCO teaching the correct precautions against triggering a trip wire. Attention changed to hilarity when the unfortunate NCO instructor accidentally set off one of his own trip flares. Later, a container of tea punctuated the morning training. No one has ever discovered the secret recipe for army tea.

The second half of the morning was devoted to first-aid training. Cries of anguish were heard from the medical instructor, who was beginning to despair after seeing his practice resuscitation doll murdered by an over-enthusiastic driver attempting to learn the principles of expired air resuscitaion.

After lunch, chemical survival skills were taught, each section spending time in turn in the tiny brick hut known as the 'gas chamber'.

On the firing ranges, a more complicated event was taking place. Having completed the very demanding annual Personal Weapons Test, each section member was required to run up a plank of wood to a window-frame, shoot at a target on the other side of the window, and then throw himself six feet down into a simulated building interior. After a theatrical demonstration by the instructor, everyone managed to perform this procedure satisfactorily, except for a young Second Lieutenant medical student, who landed badly and broke his ankle. The young officer was told to stop complaining, pick up his weapon and complete the course. Eventually his complaints were taken seriously, and the first-aid training module was put into practice three days ahead of schedule. His leg was splinted, and thereupon he experienced life in a military hospital from the casualty's viewpoint.

As the sun went down over the trees, everyone in the squadron had enjoyed a hard day's military training and, after a good dinner and some well-deserved beers, they were very happy and were looking forward to the challenges of the next day.

Compared with Vogelsang, reveille in Nijmegen was altogether more civilised. It was already 0900 hours on the first day of the Nijmegen Marches when B Squadron crawled out of their sacks and drifted towards the ablutions.

132

They had been set up in the Heumensoord Camp for several days, but today an air of excitement pervaded the squadron. Had all the training and preparation been enough, they wondered? Today would be the big test.

The Nijmegen Marches are an annual high-profile event in which 33,000 people, from all over the world, march twenty-six miles per day for four consecutive days. 3rd Armoured Field Ambulance were tasked to provide medical support to the British military contingent, which consisted of 1,500 servicemen and servicewomen from the Army and the Royal Air Force.

The main British medical facility, manned by B Squadron, consisted of a very large plastic tent supplied by the Dutch authorities. This was adapted by adding on a number of field ambulance tents, to provide a reception and documentation area and a huge waiting bay with 200 spaces available for crippled marchers. A long red carpet ran the entire length of the complex, adding a touch of regal splendour to the facility.

The marchers had hit the road before 0500 hours, and by midday they were limping back to Heumensoord, having achieved success on day one. Success at Nijmegen is measured by the ability to complete the four days as a team. Speed is irrelevant, and all teams are advised to take it slowly. There are three rest areas along the route, and B Squadron detached a section of medics to each of these areas. The sections had been hard at work since 0600 hours, and they had been very successful at keeping all the teams on the road.

Back at Heumensoord the first casualties arrived. 'It's only a small blister,' said one stoic sergeant from the RAF Regiment. However, examination of his foot showed that he had lost one-third of the skin from his heel. The sergeant hobbled along the red carpet in his flip-flops and paused alongside a line of footbaths containing a bright purple solution and cubes of ice. 'Take a seat and put your feet into that,' said a sympathetic medic. The sergeant sat down, placed his feet into the ice-cold potassium permanganate solution and heaved a euphoric sigh of relief. After a few minutes, he was led into the 'blister bunker' for some restorative treatment. The tinc benz and zinc oxide plaster treatment is the cornerstone of blister therapy; however, the sergeant's feet were so damaged that a layer of 'moleskin' had to be applied. Now a new man, the sergeant marched out gratefully, ready for another day.

By 1500 hours the atmosphere in the British Medical Facility was frenetic. The waiting area was overflowing, with more than 200 marchers anxiously expecting treatment. Two NCO drivers from the Field Ambulance were passing through the assembled ranks selling chocolates, buns and cold drinks. All the young medics worked tirelessly in the blister bunker. 'This may sting a bit, but it's good stuff,' said a new young private reassuringly, as he aimed a can of tinc benz spray at the foot of a young blonde WRAC girl. It was his first visit to Nijmegen and, although he had got his CMT 3 qualification, he had spent most of his two months at 3rd Armoured Field Ambulance checking equipment, putting up tents and doing guard duties. Now he was doing the job he was trained for, treating real patients.

At about 1600 hours an ambulance arrived outside the facility, its blue light flashing. The reception staff hurried out to meet it. It had been a very hot day and this was the first heat-stroke casualty. The unfortunate victim was wheeled directly into the major treatment area, where he was examined by the duty medical officer. He was swabbed with spirit and covered with a cold wet sheet. He was very confused, his body temperature was high and he was dehydrated. An intravenous infusion was started. On the other side of the major treatment bay was the field dental chair. A Canadian soldier with toothache was receiving expert treatment from the Field Ambulance dentist. Being the only military dentist in Nijmegen, he had willingly offered his service to all the assembled nationalities in Heumensoord camp.

In another area of the medical facility, the physiotherapy officer was hard at work; a deluge of strained joints, aching muscles and swollen feet were receiving very professional treatment with ice and ultrasound. Some of the marchers were apprehensive about this very hi-tech physiotherapy department. 'Does acupuncture hurt?' asked one marcher, who had his eyes firmly set on a placard on the other wall which read:

'PAIN IS OUR PLEASURE

AGONY IS OUR AIM'

'It's OK, doc, I'll just take an aspirin,' said another.

The evening shift of medics took over from their exhausted colleagues at 1800 hours. The work went on until the last marcher had been patched up. It was almost 2215, and 300 cases had been treated on the first day. Would they survive another three days of marching? That didn't bear thinking about. It was time to join the Zommerfest in town.

Every year, the Nijmegen Marches are accompanied by a carnival in the town. A band plays at every street corner, crowds drift from bar to beer stand to disco and back to bar. The atmosphere is relaxed and friendly as the marchers and their supporters wind down after a hard day. The field ambulance minibus ran the boys down into town, and brought them back to camp in hourly shuttles until 0300 hours.

'That was a great day,' said a happy but exhausted lance-corporal, 'and look what I've got.' With great pride he brandished a collection of Russian military insignia and cap badges, which he had swapped with an English-speaking cadet in the Soviet Army marching team. Next year it would be different; A Squadron would be supporting the marches and B Squadron would be training at Vogelsang.

A medical orderly and a nurse patch up a competitor's foot during a break in the Nijmegen Marches

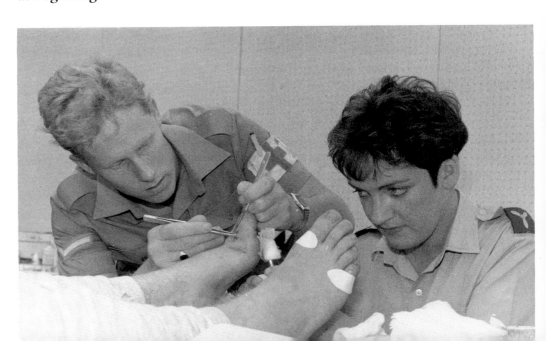

ACE Mobile Force Infantry Battalion: Royal Regiment of Fusiliers

Here we see the Royal Regiment of Fusiliers operating on the other flank of NATO with the ACE Mobile Force.

A single day is not long enough to illustrate fully the roles played, or the variety of jobs undertaken by the UK Infantry Battalion of the Allied Command Europe Mobile Force (Land) – AMF(L). However, 30 June 1989 saw the Battalion deployed on its biennial AMF(L) exercise to Denmark, hard at work alongside the other armies that make up the AMF(L).

The AMF(L) was formed in 1960 when it was decided by NATO that a show of unity amongst its members was necessary in times of international tension. It was felt that units from different countries should be brought together to form a force of brigade size (about 5,000 men), operating together under the NATO banner. The reason was that there were certain areas of Europe which were protected by the forces of only one NATO nation, and consequently these were particularly vulnerable to aggression. In the north, this meant Norway and Denmark, and in the south Italy, Greece and Turkey. It was believed that sending a NATO force to any of these areas would deter any potential aggressor from taking action.

Eight NATO countries contribute to the AMF(L): Belgium, Canada, West Germany, Italy, Luxemburg, the Netherlands, the United Kingdom, and the United States of America. There are Land (AMF(L)) and Air (AMF(A)) Forces. Luxemburg does not contribute to the Air component, but all the others contribute in some way to both. The British Army contingent includes infantry, artillery, armour, signals, and logistic units. The 2nd Battalion, Royal Regiment of Fusiliers, was then the infantry battalion in the ACE Mobile Force, and had been in that role since May 1987. Its main commitment is to the north, and thus every winter the battalion trains in Norway in Arctic Warfare. Denmark is their other northern commitment, and it is there that 2 RRF found itself on 30 June 1989.

The first part of any AMF(L) exercise is what is called 'deterrent operations'. It is considered a vital part of the mission of the AMF(L) to make an outward display of friendliness towards the population and above all to display unity within the Force itself. This involves vehicle and foot patrols, public displays, and meeting local dignitaries as well as visiting places of work and schools. Each nation provides a company of men for this task, known as Key Company.

C Company were the UK Key Company for Exercise Avenue Express, and were based in the coastal town of Holbaek, fifty kilometres west of Copenhagen. 30 June started early for those men of C Company who were out on patrol. The first vehicle patrols were out at 0600 hours, so reveille was at 0430

Men of the B Company 2 RRF Challenge Cup team approach the end of the March and Shoot competition

hours. Before setting off they have to be briefed by the Intelligence Section on their tasks for the day, and the patrol leader has to report to the Operations Room for a study of his route.

At 0600 the first patrol of eight men, led by Lieutenant Roger Thompson, rolled out of Holbaek Barracks in their two Land-Rovers on the start of their 270 kilometre round trip. They had been briefed to report in on their mobile telephone at certain checkpoints en route, and to inform the Ops Room of any suspicious incidents, but their main task was to stop and talk to locals, in order to make their presence known in as friendly a way as possible. It should be added that for the sake of building up a realistic scenario for the exercise, incidents involving 'enemy' forces are interjected. The patrols are expected to react to these, and an umpire accompanies them to see that there is fair play.

The vehicles were fired upon by two men in civilian clothes as they pulled up to a T-junction. Shots were returned, but the gunmen escaped to a nearby copse. The 2 RRF patrol gave chase, but a white car pulled away before they could reach them. The vehicle details were taken down and reported back to Holbaek immediately. The umpire was pleased with the reaction, but

Fusilier John Fergus, B
Company, having completed
the NATO Challenge Cup

'awarded' the driver of the first Land-Rover a gunshot wound to the leg and put
his vehicle out of action. This delayed the whole patrol for two hours whilst
the unfortunate driver was flown to the Field Hospital in a Gazelle helicopter
which was called out to the scene, and a REME team drove out to repair the
Land-Rover.

By now the remaining three patrols from C Company were all reporting
similar incidents. A 'landmine' destroyed one vehicle, a patrol was ambushed
as they spoke to some locals, and a foreign parachute and map were discovered on a beach after a tip-off. All did not go against the Key Company,
however; prisoners were taken at some of the incidents, some carrying vital
information. The Ops Room telephone rang continuously, and the staff were
kept busy handling reports as well as keeping HQ AMF(L) informed as to what
was going on.

The same day an early start was made by those men of A Company and Fire
Support Company who were involved in the Parade and Equipment Display at
Vaerlose Airfield near Copenhagen. At 0430 they left their tented bases in the
south of Zealand, to travel north. The early start enabled A Company to carry

137

out some drill and take part in the parade rehearsal with the other AMF(L) units. Similarly, Fire Support Company had to set up their display of mortars, anti-tank missiles and Scimitar tracked recce vehicles.

An integral part of deterrent operations, the parade and display were part of an open day for the public, designed to show the Danes who and what had flown into their country to exercise for two weeks. The Regimental Band led the parade, supported by their Italian counterparts. On a blazing hot day, in front of 15,000 people, Major-General Carstens, the German Commander of AMF(L), made a speech stressing the importance of AMF(L) operations.

Another event of 30 June which typifies life in the AMF(L) was the NATO Challenge Cup. This is a competition held during every exercise, for which all the nations enter teams. It involves an arduous ten kilometre run preceded by a long assault course, against the clock, finishing with a shoot on the firing range. The teams of twenty-six men run individually, and points are awarded for time and accuracy of shooting. With temperatures reaching 80°F, several teams dropped men through heat exhaustion, but the Germans (263 Parachute Battalion) managed a very quick time and dropped only three shots on the range. The A Company team, led by Second Lieutenant Philip Alexander, came in a minute slower but scored maximum points with their shooting and just clinched the title. After both B and C Company put in similar performances the Cup was firmly in British hands for the first time. But the rivalry was friendly enough for all teams to congratulate each other on their performances.

A Challenger Tank on exercise with the AMF. Notice the 120mm gun remains stabilised in the horizontal position whatever the angle of the chassis of the tank

In order to improve the efficiency of the Force, most units take part in 'cross training' during deterrent operations. There are shooting days when soldiers fire the rifles and machine-guns of their counterparts, and a live-firing mortar and artillery exercise is held.

In reality, deterrent operations might last for weeks or even months, but the AMF(L) must exercise as a fighting force if it is to prove its worth. On 30 June those men not involved in the parade, display or Challenge Cup were training with the Canadians, Germans and Danes. A platoon from B Company were having their own shooting competition with the Canadians and Germans. The Germans this time proved to be the better shots, but were very impressed with the new British SA-80 rifle and its optic sight. At the same time a platoon from A Company were finishing their week attached to the 1st Battalion the Danish Life Regiment, during which time they were thundering over training areas in the Danish M113 Armoured Personnel Carrier.

30 June was a busy day for the battalion, but typical for an AMF(L) exercise. In a Europe that is drawing ever closer together, 2 RRF were doing their bit.

B Company Challenge Cup team on the range at the end of the competition. They are firing the new SA-80 rifle

(Left to right) Fusiliers Wilkes,
Thompson and Morris, Lance-
Corporals Evans and Parker
preparing to spend the day
training with German troops

Around the World

17th/21st Lancers Battlegroup at BATUS

Captain P M R Daly

The British Army's largest training area is at Suffield in Canada (British Army Training Unit Suffield, or BATUS). Here, armoured battlegroups can exercise in conditions as near to real warfare as is possible in peacetime. In this instance the 17th/21st Lancers battlegroup are being put through their paces.

It is five o'clock when dawn breaks; H hour is 0600. Orders were given the previous night for an advance to contact. The battlegroup commander sits huddled inside his command vehicle with his staff officers, assessing that night's patrol reports, scanning aerial photographs and reviewing the enemy intelligence summary sent from Brigade HQ. New information forces last-minute adjustments to the plan.

Dispersed across the prairie in their hides, the squadrons and companies quietly prepare to move. Soldiers inspect their tanks and APCs. Kit is stowed, ammunition checked, weapons cleaned, and a hot brew gratefully drunk against the early morning cold.

At 0600 hours, under radio silence, the battlegroup deploys with the recce Scorpions crossing the start line to clear the advance. The battlegroup advances with two squadrons of Chieftain MBTs leading, each supported by a mechanised infantry company. On the centre line is the CO, Lieutenant-Colonel Andrew Cumming, with his Tac HQ. Behind him are the bridging and ploughing assets of the Engineer Troop. Further back, strung out behind Battlegroup Headquarters, come the logistic support vehicles required to keep the cutting edge sharp; the long tail of the armoured animal.

The advance progresses swiftly. Minor enemy detachments are located and bypassed by the squadrons. The infantry companies deal with them as they follow through. No point in being diverted by minor sideshows. Stick to the mission, maintain momentum and save the punch for the knockout blow. These are the philosophies the CO has instilled into his battlegroup. Forward in his tank he is practising what he preaches: controlling, directing, cajoling. A small minefield is located and breached, with minor opposition; the battlegroup filters through the safelanes ploughed and marked by the engineers.

Suddenly Recce Troop come under fire. They return fire with their 76 mm guns, withdraw slightly and probe again, trying to ascertain exactly where the enemy is and in what strength. It appears to be a large force, so the battlegroup commander issues a warning order for a quick attack. Recce helicopters are

called in to help identify the threat. A dug-in company of infantry with BMP and tank support is identified, and the details are passed to the commander. It calls for a full-scale battlegroup attack.

Orders are sent rapidly over the radio; speed of response increases the shock of an attack. C Squadron sends a tank troop to each company. The remaining half squadron moves to a position to shoot the attack in. A Squadron will lead the assault, and both companies are given specific objectives to take out. The Battery Commander, Major John Gibbon, produces a fireplan for the artillery. Milan anti-tank weapons are despatched to secure the flanks.

Just forty-five minutes from the initial contact, and A Squadron's Chieftain tanks, led by Major Patrick Marriot, are making their way across the battlefield and into the assault. A thunderous artillery bombardment sends the enemy down into cover as shrapnel, white phosphorus and high explosive fall around the positions. From a flank, the Chieftains in fire support provide even more destruction. Closed down, fourteen tanks charge towards the enemy line abreast – the modern-day cavalry in action.

This Chieftain has been hit by a Simfire laser beam which has activated a smoke discharger fixed to each tank. This signifies that the tank has been 'hit' and that it is therefore out of the exercise. The Simfire system adds enormous realism to an exercise

From inside the tank turret the picture is not so clear. One commander, Staff Sergeant Snelling, struggles to see through the small, dirty sights in his cupola to ensure his rate of advance and direction are correct. Anxiously he strains to locate the enemy armour or other anti-tank weapons. The gunner, Trooper Ahrens, his head hard against the sight, views the battle through two small eye-pieces. When he spots the enemy he flicks to times ten magnification, lays on the gun and fires. Through the intense obscuration of dust and smoke he sees a bright flash. Target destroyed. He scans for another kill. Fired up, he shouts into his sight as he lays on to another enemy tank and presses the firing switch. Another flash, another kill. Impersonal but deadly. In the other side of the turret the loader, Lance-Corporal Taylor, sweats as he heaves another kinetic energy round into the breech, pushes the charge in behind, rams the vent tube, shuts the breech, makes the guard. Ready. The gun recoils as another round finds its mark at over 1,500 metres per second. Dust and fumes fill the turret as he reloads. A round every twelve seconds. The crew coughs and splutters, momentarily no one can see anything. The driver, Trooper Bus, his visibility obscured by the splash all around, tries to choose the smoothest terrain, to give his gunner the most stable firing platform, talking him through every bump and gear change. It's this close co-operation required to fight a tank well, and the cramped, uncomfortable conditions inside the turret, that foster the intimate bonds of a tank crew.

Together the Chieftains assault through the position. Most of the enemy armour has been destroyed; the remainder is withdrawing rapidly. With the threat from hand-held anti-tank weaons into their flanks now high, the commander fires his smoke grenades and puts searching machine-gun fire into possible firing posts. Through the objective into the unknown – where are the enemy now? The tanks push on aggressively, seeking out more enemy to destroy before securing the next bound, ready to repulse any counter-attack.

The intimate support troops follow up the initial armoured assault, the troop leader relaying as much information as he can about enemy trench positions. It is not easy amid the confusion of burning vehicles, mutilated bodies, small arms fire in all directions, dust and smoke billowing everywhere. But the tanks lead the APCs on to their objectives, using their machine-guns to force the enemy back into cover now the artillery has ceased pummelling the position.

It is the turn of the infantry. The APCs lurch forward and stop. More dust envelops the vehicles as the back doors swing open, discharging men of No 3 Company Grenadier Guards at the double. They shake out and skirmish forward in their fire-teams. Section commanders struggle to keep control amid the noise and confusion of battle. Crawling towards the trenches the grenades go in. In pairs the Guardsmen rush forward and clear what is left. The discipline and teamwork are faultless. It is a methodical, clinical and bloody operation. When the objective is secure the APCs will return to collect their weary charges and transport them across the battlefield to their next task.

The attack has been a success. Casualties were light – the weight of fire had done its job. The wounded are given first aid, intravenous drips to prevent shock, and taken back to the Regimental Aid Post by ambulance. It stops at Battlegroup Headquarters to hand over a captured enemy map. The Intelligence Cell examine it and pass on the crucial information – it has other enemy locations marked.

As the reorganisation is consolidated, the CO receives fresh orders over the secure radio. On the modern battlefield events move quickly. Intelligence reports an armoured column moving south to reinforce the routed motor rifle regiment. A major counter-attck is expected during the night. The battlegroup is to hold Copse Hollow and destroy the enemy.

The battlegroup commander calls an 'O' group and together with his operations officer, Captain Mark Horlock, finalises the intricate detail required to fight a successful defensive battle: hide locations, fireplan, timings, target acquisition, electronic security, policy on light for a night battle, different anti-armour options.

While orders are given, logistic vehicles move up to replenish the tanks and APCs with fuel and ammunition. The fitters take advantage of the lull to repair damaged vehicles, track down recurring faults, and ensure every tank and APC is battleworthy. Tank crews carry out essential maintenance to the tracks,

A 17th/21st Chieftain crew prepare to break cover to advance across the Suffield training area in Canada to mount a live firing attack on an objective some miles away

Infantry supporting the 17th/21st Lancers deploying into battle positions at BATUS

engines and gun kit. Weapons are cleaned, a quick meal cooked. The infantry dig in. Those who can, grab some sleep. When the CO's orders are over there will be more battle procedure to carry out: concealment, recces, patrols, deception.

* * *

It is not for real. However, at BATUS it is as close as it can be. There are twelve hundred square miles of unrestricted prairie to exercise across, targetry to simulate Soviet attack formations, and the narrowest safety margins permissible for peacetime live firing. Were it for real, the location would be the North German Plains, the tanks the latest Challenger MBTs, the infantry mounted in the new Warrior AFVs and the firepower greater. Massive Soviet artillery bombardments would replace the battle simulations, and the ensuing casualties would not come back to life. For the 17th/21st Lancers and all the attached arms that make up an armoured battlegroup it is the most extensive and realistic training for war they can ever experience.

Night has fallen. The glimmer of the northern lights shines across the sky, and shadows play tricks on tired eyes. Enemy recce is probing forward. It is going to be a long night. It has already been a long day.

146

A Day in the Life of 29 Commando Regiment Royal Artillery

The Gunners provide the fire support for the Army. Here we see 29 Commando Regiment Royal Artillery spread all over the world on 30 June 1989.

The sun has crept over the high jungle trees. A hummingbird flits from flower to flower on the balcony, and a chit-chat runs up the wall. What a far cry from normal life in Plymouth. Today is Friday 30 June 1989 and 8 (Alma) Commando Battery have completed three months of a six-month tour in Belize. The rest of the regiment are spread far and wide.

7 (Sphinx) Commando Battery are on a period of adventure training, with expeditions in Scotland and one in the Lake District. Those who are left in Arbroath are taking part in a parachuting and abseiling programme. 79 (Kirkee) Commando Battery are at Wainwright in Canada with 2nd Battalion the Light Infantry, and 148 (Meiktila) Commando Forward Observation Battery are hosting a party of United States Marine Corps soldiers on an exercise around Cape Wrath. 289 Commando Battery (Volunteers) are having a weekend off. They have just returned from a two-week camp in Gibraltar, and next weekend they will be off to Salisbury Plain to practise deploying guns from helicopters. For the remainder of the regiment in Plymouth there will be a free weekend, unless there is a guard duty to perform or they are involved in a demonstration at one of the local schools.

29 Commando Regiment Royal Artillery is the 'Gunner' unit that supports 3 Commando Brigade Royal Marines. The regiment is based in a number of locations scattered around the British Isles. The largest element, comprising Regimental Headquarters, 8 (Alma) Commando Battery, 79 (Kirkee) Commando Battery, Headquarters Battery and the Light Aid Detachment from the Royal Electrical and Mechanical Engineers, is based in the Royal Citadel which stands on the east end of Plymouth Hoe. The detached batteries are 7 (Sphinx) Commando Battery, who live at Arbroath in Scotland, 148 (Meiktila) Commando Forward Observation Battery, who are based at Poole in Dorset, and 289 Commando Battery (Volunteers), who reside in East London.

Each of the numbered batteries, apart from 148 battery, is equipped with six 105 mm Light Guns. 148 Battery is a grouping of specialist observation parties who provide the 'eyes' to direct naval gunfire from ship to shore. Headquarters Battery, apart from containing those whose job it is to administer the rest of the regiment, is also the home of a troop of three Cymbeline Mortar Locating Radars.

Typical of 8 Battery's activities in Belize were those of a small patrol of five of

(Previous page) A Sea King helicopter moving a 105mm Light Gun to a near position

its members. At midday on 30 June they are having a wash and clean-up next to a cool river pool. A bombardier is the patrol commander, and he has with him three gunners from the battery and a member of the Belize Defence Force, who acts as the interpreter. The patrol have been out in the jungle for five days and have another two to go. Their task is to visit a number of villages and to keep an eye on tracks that lead to the border with Guatemala. Given the present relaxation of tension on the border, anyone they meet is much more likely to be engaged in drug smuggling than military activity. In the main, the patrol is carrying out a 'hearts and minds' operation, making sure that all is well in the very cut-off villages they visit. The patrol is hard work, with difficult terrain to cross and 60-lb bergen rucksacks to carry. However, they have all enjoyed the real challenge and considerable responsibility they have been given, and the chance to put into practice all they have learned on their three-week jungle warfare course.

7 Battery in Scotland does not have many soldiers in camp, mainly due to the adventure training expeditions, but partly because some are away on a tour with 42 Commando Royal Marines, or else with 8 Battery in Belize. The expeditions have been organised by the junior NCOs of the battery, overseen by a sergeant and the Battery Training Officer. The result is that today there are parties cycling round Scotland, climbing on the Isle of Skye, canoeing on the River Spey, and climbing and walking in the Lake District. In Arbroath, twelve recruits who are shortly to start the Commando course have joined the remainder of the battery for a day of abseiling and, for those who are qualified, parachuting. The training is to be done from one of the Royal Navy's Sea King helicopters. It will start after drills for the parachutists and abseiling for the recruits from the top of a dry ski slope, a vertical drop of fifty feet. By the end of the day the parachutists will have completed four or five jumps, and the abseilers descents of 200 feet.

Today is also the start of 148 Battery's joint exercise with the Air and Naval Gunfire Liaison and Control (ANGLICO) teams from the USMC. The plan is to emplane at Hurne Airport near Bournemouth and to carry out a parachute jump into the water of Loch Eriboll on the north coast of Scotland. The 'P' hour is 0600 hours, and after a recovery by the battery's Gemini inflatable boats the five-man teams have to move on foot, carrying all their kit and radios, to set up an observation post overlooking an enemy radar station. This entails a seven-mile cross-country march and a crossing of the River Dionard.

79 Battery in Canada are due to fire in support of an infantry company attack. They plan to deploy to an initial position close to the company's start line so that the soldiers of 2 LI can visit to see what goes on. A series of fire missions will signify the start of the company's advance towards the enemy. When the leading troops are in the right position the battery will follow its fireplan. This will engage known enemy locations, and assist the Company Commander in achieving his mission of destroying the enemy. After dark a night battle will be practised, with the guns firing illuminating rounds as well as high explosive.

Gunners provide the main fire support for the Army and Commando Brigade world wide. 30 June 1989 was no exception for 29 Commando Regiment Royal Artillery.

(Overleaf) All soldiers, including gunners, have to train in basic infantry techniques. Here a gunner does a turn at sentry duty behind a Light Support Weapon

Battlegroup South at Rideau Camp, Belize: 9 Parachute Squadron Royal Engineers

Captain B Sinclair RE

*The Royal Engineers are jacks of all trades. Here Captain Ben Sinclair
of 9 Parachute Squadron Royal Engineers vividly describes how his
sappers built a camp in the jungle in Belize – not all on 30 June!*

Some mornings I lie awake, just before the alarm goes off at 0550, and watch the early light breaking through the canopy. Dawn and dusk are rapid events here in the tropics, separated by almost exactly twelve hours of light each day.

Alone with the darkness, the nocturnal noises of the bush have died away, replaced by a short period of calm, which will last a few minutes. Then the day begins with a gradual increase in volume, commensurate with the intensity of light. Numerous birds in the canopy around the camp chirrup, chortle and hack. An early ground mist – soon to disappear – offers false promise of cool air.

The sun rises just after 0600, though the camp is in the shadow of Saddleback Hill's twin peaks for another hour. A sudden rapid movement, dress in a few minutes, and out for a swift gathering of the troop. Few words are spoken.

Physical training at 0600 is not the most popular of activities. However, the heat of the day, combined with a busy programme, dictates this use of the early hours. Here a little imagination is required. This morning I decide to climb Saddleback, as on the hill I can beat most of the young whippets who would beat me on the flat, and I need a photograph from the top.

The troop runs out on to the only road – more of a farm track, really, like most in Belize, unmetalled and muddy from rain. Clad in boots, denims and maroon vest, a regular beat of feet with an easy rhythm as we head down the road for three-quarters of a mile. Then a sudden sharp left through apparently impenetrable secondary jungle, and a sprint up the hill as fast as possible all the way. A 45° slope, mud, slippery limestone, rotten vegetation and much groaning. Hopefully the noise will clear any beasties from the track; climbing hand and foot, the front runners must hope to avoid any snakes or scorpions in the convenient handholds. Twenty minutes later at the top, in a lungbusting climb – arriving a good fifteen yards ahead of the next man – good!

A quick photo of warm, determined faces, and a panoramic shot of the sea, south to the Guatemalan and Honduran coastlines. Salient features of the terrain are pointed out to a couple of newcomers, then off across the Saddle to the opposite peak. Running downhill at speed over rough terrain leads to fun and falls, and a heightened awareness of the ubiquitous bastard tree that reaches out, to impale any hand grasping for a hold on a bed of needles. It is cool under the canopy, though the high humidity results in dripping wet bodies, each man's temperature rising by the minute.

Again upward, over harsh, shattered rock, opening out on to the peak fifteen minutes later, this time overlooking the camp from a sheer cliff. To the west are the foothills of the Cockscomb Mountains – just visible in the haze, rising like dinosaurs from the swampy plain, with the Guatemalan border forty miles distant. A short rest – every man is now well awake, and witty remarks crack the air. The sun is up, shirts steam in its heat. Then down the hill, short cut down a flash flood route – almost vertical – at speed, very muddy and wet, to the fields at the back of Rideau Camp. Descent in six minutes. One young lad lost on the way down and a couple caught in the barbed wire perimeter fence as they attempt a short cut into camp. However, all are gathered in, swift shower and breakfast just after 0700. For the boys, a scrum in the cookhouse as they compete (successfully) with the infantry for the food, while I ease into the Officers' Mess – a delightful set-up outside, on a veranda covered with a palm leaf Attap roof, complete with lizards and occasional tarantulas, and enjoy a quiet half-hour with a five-day-old paper and a cup of tea.

The day's work proper starts at 0800 – a luxury today; the last couple of days, the cement mixer has dictated an 0600 start. The boys muster at 0755 and the machinery starts on the hour. The troop at Rideau is in the process of building six prefabricated buildings on large concrete bases, with a production schedule of three at a time, all to be completed in three months. At first glance no problem, though time slips by with the logistics of moving all stores – cement, timber, glass, roofing, reinforcing wire, paint, tiles, electrical stores and much more – by ship from Belize City in the north. There is no luxury of readymix here, and the nearest suitable quarry for aggregate is 200 miles away by very rough road!

Today building No 1 is up, now in the process of being decorated inside and electrical fittings installed. No 2 is assembled like an outsize Meccano set. However, No 3 will take the most time today. Metal roadforms and timber formwork are in place, accurately sited with a theodolite yesterday by Corporal Buttery and his section. Today the concrete is to be poured – a continuous process incorporating ring beam and three slabs, that will finish sometime tonight between 2100 and midnight. Brown bodies hang like monkeys on a climbing frame – now well acclimatised to the sun's heat, the boys throw the metal cladding on to the steel superstructure with speed, dexterity and great noise. At the same time a chain gang of six is busy working up at the concrete batching site mixing concrete with a 400-litre machine, throwing out a mix every six minutes or so at best performance. Cubes have been taken for strength testing, and now the site produces an incessant stream of concrete porridge, transported down to the building base where it is poured into the framework and set upon by soldiers wielding shovels and vibrating pokers. The fair weather looks as if it will hold – it's heartbreaking laying sixteen cubic metres of concrete in a morning, and watching a tropical rainstorm wash the top four inches off into the storm drains.

The construction of these buildings is dealt with practically by the troop, commanded by Corporals Buttery, Prest and Glover, with quality control from myself and Staff Sergeant 'George' Askwith, with whom I run the troop. A very valuable man, steady, with a dry sense of humour, almost essential when dealing either with the erratic supply line, and those who control the logistical side up in Belize City, or with the sometimes quite unfathomable activities of some members of the troop.

As the immediate taskmasters, both of us are frequent targets of much caustic but friendly (usually) humour, mostly unrepeatable. We control the provision of all stores and materials and the organisation of what happens where – the work we both manage to extract is, to me, quite extraordinary. No civilian contractor could (or would) work with such intensity over an extended period of time, and for the same wage, back in England. Such is the nature of the British soldier. At about 1000 hours the troop stop work briefly for an ice-cold 'stim' (a peculiar word, military slang for a soft drink). Otherwise they work on through to lunch at 1230. Having the luxury of a small fridge in my office – stolen last month from one of the next-door Gunner officers – saves me the hassle of walking back to the Mess. Up in our own unofficial bar at the Engineer end of the camp lives Fluff, a six-foot boa constrictor of friendly disposition. Lance-Corporal McLean, a diminutive Scotsman, looks after the reptile, and if I've half an hour or so free I'll go up and play with her. Feeding is due any day now – usually a chicken or some small animal – an activity bound to draw a crowd, as Fluff dispatches her victim with impressive speed. Normally we feed her once every two weeks, so she is sufficiently motivated to consume immediately – though it is not unusual to see a chicken sitting on the head of an unconcerned snake!

In the hours before lunch there occurs a very important aspect of life for the British soldier serving on foreign soil. A siren goes off in the Battalion headquarters on the other side of camp, signifying the arrival of mail. This arrives by light plane from Belize City 240 miles away, flown daily or near daily (depending upon the importance of other cargo – a priority we are unable to assign). Mail for all out here is of paramount importance. The effect of the arrival (or not, according to fortune) of apparently insignificant quantities of paper on the morale of men abroad is dramatic, and one of the most important aspects of personal spirit on a day-to-day basis. I have seen men waste away as they await a non-existent letter from home. Unfortunately, few back home seem to realise the importance of letters, however mundane and ordinary. I find that an average investment of twenty letters will give me a return of four or five – somehow the pleasure of reception doesn't prompt the drudgery of literary composition. No mail for me today!

Lunch is often a social event, with outsiders dropping in – passing pilots and other one-day visitors from the unpopular base camp in the north. By now the sun is directly overhead, though the Mess, surrounded by tall green hyacinth bushes, complete with attendant tiny green hummingbirds, is visually cool to the eye, if not physically to the skin.

Back on the job just after 1300 with a deadline to meet, the camp resounds to the sounds of construction – cement mixers grinding, chisel and hammer,

Sappers of 9 Parachute
Squadron Royal Engineers
laying the concrete base for a
hut at Rideau Camp in Belize

the screech of drilled concrete as pinion bolts are prepared for grouting in. Concrete tiles, 800 per building to be laid, taking two men three days' slow grind.

Just before 1400, two of the corporals head off down to the local town of Punta Gorda on an obscure mission to one of the many wooden churches. Relations with the locals here are good. Punta Gorda is a small, essentially Caribbean town with a large Afro-Caribbean and Garifundi population. Though the town lacks many of the amenities we take for granted in a village in the UK, it is vibrant, cheerful and full of life. These two reprobates, Corporals Buttery (a juvenile version of Alf Garnett) and Prest (a touch more refined), have been invited by a local family to become godparents at the christening of their child. I find it impossible to imagine these two hairy-arsed sappers being responsible for the moral welfare and upbringing of a babe in arms.

At the same time I take a Gazelle helicopter out into the wilds of the Cockscomb Mountains, another thirty miles inland. The troop continues working under the beady eye of Staff Sergeant Askwith, whilst I have to recce a site for an exercise in the coming weeks. This will involve the use of explosives, both for battle simulation and to clear an LZ (landing zone) out in the bush. It is far quicker to remove trees by explosive than by hand, though a degree of thought is required.

The chopper, piloted by a friend, Lieutenant Richard Bamber AAC, flies high over the flat coastal plain to the hills. During the flight we encounter three separate rainstorms – a new micro-climate every four to five kilometres or so. Clouds brush the mountains, and the ravages of the *milpas* (slash and burn) agricultural system in inhabited areas are clearly seen below. Much of Belize is now secondary jungle, with thick areas of low brush, tall grasses and palm trees. However, up in the deep forest in the hills it is a quite magical experience, even if torrential rain can obliterate everything for hours on end.

This trip also has a special relevance, as in a month's time I will be sending out two five-man patrols each week into this green wilderness, over a period of three weeks. We will be taking over the patrol duties for the infantry, who will be handing over to another unit later in the month. Each patrol must carry everything it needs for its task, though they will be resupplied with food by helicopter at the four-day point. So time must be set aside in the next few weeks for preparation – first aid, use of high-frequency radio, emergency procedure and radio location – as well as putting some rounds down the small range at the side of Rideau. The troop has been fortunate in that we have put most of our boys through a ten-day jungle warfare course, a few at a time. This was run by other members of the squadron at a patrol base up in the hills near Salamanca Camp. Lieutenant Brian Hemmings runs that show – when he is not swanning around back at Belize City – taking groups of twenty every twelve days. Brian comes out of the bush every so often in varying states of disrepair. He may well be coming down tonight if he can hitch a lift, and the dizzy lights and eating houses of Punta Gorda will be this evening's objective.

I arrive back at Rideau at 1630 hours and spend the next half-hour on site before the boys have their tea. The transformation in just one day's work is startling; with every man heavily involved, the new building has shot up, and

Lance-Corporal 'Mac' McLean
of 9 Parachute Squadron
reading a letter from home.
Everything stops for the mail

154

much of the concrete for the third base is now laid. Sapper Yates, with more emulsion on his body than on his brush, enthusiastically decorates one of the timber doors, while Sapper Jarvis completes his tenth set of casement windows, complete with reinforced glazing.

For a reason I have never been able to fathom, the military persists in feeding its men their evening meal at an early hour. At 1700 the camp quietens down as the masses are fed – traditional English food, chips with everything, even in this most tropical of locations. Good reasons are always found for why local food cannot be used, mainly because of irregular supply – however, lighter meals would be appreciated in this heat. The Officers' and Sergeants' Messes both eat later in the day, at a civilised hour, but for the remainder, the last they see of food is at about 1710 hours. This accounts for the popularity of some of Punta Gorda's less than passable eating houses!

Straight after the meal, most of the troop are back on task – the sun has yet to go down. Two Bedford trucks roll out of the camp gate on their way to the Rio Grande river, where they will pick up a boat patrol that has been out for the past two days. The troop here incorporates a boat section that runs six Rigid Raider craft, powered by Johnson 140-hp engines, for patrols at sea and up the four main rivers in the south. As much of southern Belize is without a good road system, the waterways are often the most reliable routes inland. The longest, the Sarstoon river, forms the southern border with Guatemala. This river extends forty miles inland to the extreme south-west of the country and the boat section frequently takes infantry patrols, in three or four boats, in an overt expression of presence, for the benefit of any Guatemalan observers.

Back in camp, some of the boys who are not directly employed on the construction side have gone down to the emergency water supply tanks for a quick dip – a luxury to immerse in totally fresh water, though not long enough for a proper swim. The nearest bath is 240 miles away, and showers are boring after five months.

Fluff appreciates a swim as well – Lance-Corporal McLean sometimes takes her down, effectively solving the overcrowding problem. It is strange how some people are not bothered by snakes, and others will run a mile.

From 1730 hours the shadows extend and the air cools slightly. With the sun disappearing just after 1800 hours, the light soon begins to fail – by 1840 hours it is as black as midnight. As the dark swamps the atmosphere, so the forest noises change, with roosting parrots and other birds arguing over sites in the trees. The camp settles into its night routine – guards change at the gate, and most of the local civilian workers leave, walking back to town. Only on site does work go on – the troop labours on under the intense light of a large lighting tower. The work is very much in the hands of the three corporals. Little office work can be done, as most agencies have closed down, and what the troop achieves at this hour is self motivated. The concrete still pours forth from the mixer, like a dinosaur with dysentery, and the last mix goes in place just after 2100 hours. Then mixer and dumper trucks are swilled out, licked inside and out with old engine oil, while the rapidly setting slab is knocked into shape. Tonight work finished at the average time. Some days a natural break is found at 1700 hours; the latest so far was 0215 hours.

Sappers of 9 Parachute Squadron keeping up to date with their weapon training and fieldcraft in Belize

156

The sight of sappers working initially drew looks of surprise from the infantry, but they've now grown used to the idea, and consider all sappers to be a little insane – not necessarily a bad image in a world where individuality results in independence from the common herd, and the luxury of being left alone!

Brian Hemmings arrives in camp, on 'my' 500 cc Armstrong DR (Despatch Rider) motorcycle, which he stole a week ago. I thought he had broken it, but I learn on the grapevine that he ran out of petrol half-way to Salamanca, and had to run the fifteen miles back. Teach him to take a bike at night without checking the fuel! I am honoured to find he has declined dinner with a local nun, to go out with me and hit Punta Gorda. At 2130 hours we roll out of camp in a Land-Rover, and drive down to the town, taking a bumpy short cut over the municipal airstrip. The choice is limited: either the Kowloon, a restaurant run by a Chinese girl called Suzi Mak in a wooden shed with a single light bulb and tin tables, or the Miramar, a large Chinese restaurant on the high street, currently out of bounds. The Miramar wins it, as I went to Suzi's last week and the Miramar should be fairly quiet. After a good meal and a couple of the local beers from the Belikin brewery, known by most as 'bellyache' – the best in Belize and one of the worst in Central America – the local Mahogany bar across the way emits a subconscious appeal. Adopted by the troop it has become 'our' bar, a singularly grotty dark and damp place that sells food of a dubious nature and looks out on to the harbour at the point where most of the town's waterborne rubbish ends up. Its appearance is somewhat improved by the fact that only one low red bulb is working. Brian tries to make himself understood by talking Swahili to a Creole-speaking girl, not helped by the sound of a cassette recorder blasting out a unique form of music known as Punta rock. He is not put out in the least, as he is rarely understood by a girl at the best of times – in fact, he quite enjoys himself.

We both pull out at 0030 and get back to camp in a swirl of dust, heading straight for bed. PT tomorrow morning has been put on hold as the RPL (Ramp Powered Lighter) is arriving at Punta Gorda Pier at 0530 and the stores will have to be off-loaded as soon as she docks.

As I roll into bed, the quiet of the night is broken as the heavens open and the water pours out of the sky, filling the storm drains in seconds and beating a crazy rhythm on the corrugated iron roof. The noise makes no difference – I sleep.

The Royal Signals with the UN in Namibia

The Royal Signals provide most of the communications for the Army. Here we see them in Namibia providing the communications for the UN force there.

0001 Hours, Windhoek

Another starlit night in Namibia. Deployed from 30th Signal Regiment with the United Nations, overseeing the transition of Namibia to independence, Corporal Brian Croxford and his four-man shift are working in the communication centre (COMMCEN for short). They await the influx of daily situation reports from the many detachments scattered around the country.

The COMMCEN is based in Windhoek, the capital of Namibia, and from here spreads a spider's web of radio and telephone links throughout the coun-

30 Signal Regiment pose for one for the album before embarking for UN duty in Namibia

try, and ultimately as far as Cyprus and the UK. This is the nerve centre for the day's activities for the whole of our 175-man contingent. It contains high-frequency radio sets which form links from the Angolan border in the north to the South African border in the south. Some of these links serve man-portable, voice-only stations, but most are to vehicle-mounted teleprinter terminals. A small computer masterminds the system, enabling all the traffic to be easily co-ordinated and passed to the staff in the UN headquarters with the minimum of fuss. There is also a telephone switchboard and long-range radio equipment which provide a link to Cyprus and from there into the worldwide defence communications system, giving us an 'umbilical cord' to the UK. During his twelve-hour shift, Brian has to control this hive of activity. At midnight, with all yesterday's traffic sent, things are becoming more peaceful. Over the next few hours the situation reports will come in from UN units and our own detachments, and the shift will log and file them for the staff to action later.

0530 Oshakati

Eight hundred kilometres north of Windhoek, Lieutenant Joe Cooper has given up trying to sleep. Sporadic gunshots from the local township have kept him awake most of the night, although from the sound of Staff Sergeant Bob Petrie and the lads, they could be back home tucked up in their beds. Feeling very sticky with the heat, he has a cold shower to wake himself up.

0630 Swakopmund

A town located on the cold, misty Atlantic coast. Lance-Corporal Mick Sim, one of the five men running this detachment, has just finished typing and sending his situation report to the COMMCEN in Windhoek. Reading and deciphering these various reports can provide hours of endless fun, with contributions coming from Danish, Canadian, Bangladeshi and Finnish UN representatives, all using this, the only real means of communication back to the UN HQ in Windhoek. It's time to put the kettle on and to attempt to persuade the other four to leave their sleeping bags. While they are preparing to venture out of the tent, Mick starts to cook a breakfast of army compo ration sausages and beans. That task complete, someone will replace him on the radio and he can retire to bed and catch up on a missed night's sleep.

0800 Windhoek

Back in the COMMCEN the day shift has taken over from Corporal Croxford and his crew, and already the Commanding Officer is coming in and dealing with his signals. All the sitreps have been dealt with, and the quartermaster's department is even now loading a four-ton Bedford truck to take all the requested resupply forward to Grootfontein.

Lieutenant Joe Cooper's voice breaks through the static on the command radio from Oshakati, as he informs the COMMCEN that he is about to start his daily troop visits around his detachments along the Angolan border. His troop is spread over an area larger than Wales, and at each detachment he will offer advice, sort out any problems and deliver much-needed supplies, ranging from communications equipment to rations, fuel, mail and newspapers.

The Keetmanshoop detachment send in a very lengthy report from the Irish military observers, saying the first of today's military convoys returning to South Africa has passed through their location. The COMMCEN log its arrival and then redirect it to the relevant members of the staff at the UN HQ.

0854 Ondangwa

Corporal Harry Mullen is working at the Ongwadiva camp run by the United Nations High Commission for Refugees (UNHCR). At very short notice we volunteered to help UNHCR by providing two-man radio operator teams at a number of their camps to provide communication cover for the repatriation of some 38,000 refugees into Namibia, mainly from Angola and Zambia. Harry is in one of these teams and now works on a radio net that stretches around Namibia and as far as Luanda and Geneva. Without good communications, co-ordination of the movement of all these refugees would be impossible. All the equipment has been purpose-bought off the shelf by UNHCR, and is a far cry from our usual Army kit. Working in a civilian atmosphere, the boys have been forced to adapt from Army voice procedures to requests and answers last heard on *Z Cars* – the latest: 'Hello Ongwadiva, it's Shirley from Luanda, can you ask Denis to meet me for dinner on Sunday?' Still, it's great to be working in such a different environment and doing such a worthwhile job.

1030 Windhoek

The resupply stores are all loaded, and the four-tonner driven by Corporal Jed Astell and Signalman Trevor Paisey, both Driver Electricians, sets off for the forward logistic base at Grootfontein. It is a 550-kilometre drive, and their ETA is 1830 hours. The UN Headquarters is now at full tilt, with around 100 staff officers from five continents of the world, generating signals detailing the orders for the 4,600 troops on the ground. All these messages are passed over our radio links, and all must pass through the COMMCEN. By now the shift is also dealing with a steady flow from the Ministry of Defence in the UK. Busy would be an understatement.

1143 Windhoek

Crisis. The COMMCEN computer suddenly stops working. Corporal Mick Swift, the duty technician, is called, and two minutes later he is up to his eyes in a spaghetti of cables and leads. He is being called all the names under the sun by a frustrated shift, who are watching the work pile up. Methodically he starts to try to locate the fault. 1210: crisis over. Corporal Swift has replaced two circuit boards, and the computer is back. Thankful a suitable miracle has been performed, the shift start to battle against the backlog of signals.

1300 Ondangwa

After spending four hours manhandling 400 lb of antenna 700 feet up a mast, two Royal signals riggers, Sergeant Andy Tempest and Lance-Corporal Mac McCleary, decide to stop for lunch. It is exceedingly hot, 39°C, and the climb was very exhausting. They clip themselves on securely and start to relax. It's at this point that they start to search through their packs for lunch – but to no

Making friends in Namibia

(Opposite) A signalman serving with the UN force in Namibia

Men of the Royal Signals use high ground as a radio relay station in Namibia

avail. Two minutes later the sandwich box is spotted, 700 feet below. There's a deadly silence and then Mac says, 'Well, I carried it up yesterday.'

1325 Opuwo

Right in the heart of Kaokoland, surrounded by Stone Age tribesmen. Signalman Nigel Brewin, part of a two-man detachment with a manpack radio and a satellite terminal, is attempting to pass a message for the Yugoslavian police monitors. They seem totally confused, and so with the utmost diplomacy, and in his best pidgin English, Signalman Brewin tries to explain the facilities available on the terminal. He keeps his patience even though he has explained it all many times before; perhaps this time they will at last understand – one never knows one's luck.

1510 Rundu

On the Angolan border the five-man detachment are having their fortnightly visit from the paymaster and doctor. At last more money and more anti-malarial tablets. None of this administration is allowed to interfere with the passing of messages back to Windhoek, co-ordinating the daily flying schedules of the Spanish and Italian Air Forces, which are both based here at Rundu airfield.

1630 Windhoek

The major event of the day: last Monday's mail and newspapers arrive.

1800 Eenhana

Three soldiers, all radio relay operators by trade, are attempting to get the local tactical microwave telephone system working. For a few days they have been sorting out the equipment left behind by the South African Defence Force, and now at last they are ready to do the final engineering on the link. Once the system is working the Eenhana UN electoral staff will at last be able to use a telephone to contact their office in Windhoek.

1900 Windhoek

Corporal Brian Croxford and his shift are back at work on the last of their three night shifts. Tomorrow it's three days off, and he is taking his shift off into the Namib Desert to explore the area and to attempt to climb the highest mountain in Namibia – but first, twelve hours' work.

1910 Grootfontein

Five hundred and fifty kilometres and a flat tyre later, Corporal Astell and Signalman Paisey in the four-ton Bedford roll into Grootfontein. A long, hot, tiring day, but now their job is completed, it's time for a shower, a meal and a much-longed-for beer.

2157 Windhoek

Over the national emergency net the COMMCEN suddenly hears a call for help. There has been a serious car accident involving a UN vehicle, and its driver has radioed in on the emergency frequency to ask for assistance. Two of his passengers are injured, one very seriously. Out here there are no 999 calls to emergency services; it's all up to the COMMCEN shift to organise.

2159 Hours

Corporal Croxford rings the duty staff officer at the headquarters, to inform him of the accident. Then he telephones the Swiss medical unit to alert the duty doctor.

2206 Hours

A message is flashed by radio to Rundu, and the Italian helicopter is scrambled and on the way.

2209 Hours

Corporal Croxford then informs the UN Police, but the accident is seventy kilometres away from the nearest police station. The chopper will reach the scene first.

2210 Hours

As far as Corporal Croxford and the shift are concerned, that is all they can do to help, it is up to the UN emergency services to cope now.

2300 Hours

Having made a brew, the COMMCEN shift finish off yesterday's traffic and at last have time to read a book or contemplate life. COMMCENs and Radio Detachments all around the world, whether they are in a tent in a field or in a smart air-conditioned office, maintain twenty-four hours a day communications 365 days a year, and in this dusty corner of the world called Namibia no exception is made. Still, in one hour it's the first of July, and who knows what's in store for us all?

No two days are the same in the Royal Signals, especially when you are on a UN operation in the middle of Africa. There is such a variety of trades, and the only thing that one can be certain about is that any one day will see all these tradesmen working together as a team – everyone has to rely on each other and good teamwork is the key to success. Out here, working in such a harsh environment with so many nationalities, the challenge of providing a professional communications system is even greater than normal. It is very rewarding to be doing a real job, and to be part of an organisation with the vitally important task of overseeing Namibia's transition to independence.

Gurkhas form the bulk of the
garrison in Hong Kong. Here
two Gurkha soldiers are seen
on patrol in the border area
with China

Exercise Blue Flyer: The Gurkhas Visit Australia

The famed Gurkhas, so loyal to the British Crown for many years, still form a vital part of the British Infantry. Here they train in Australia.

Exercise Blue Flyer 89 was the anti-tank concentration for Milan platoons from 48 Brigade, and was held in Victoria, Australia. During the seven-week exercise Milan platoons stationed in Hong Kong from 2/2, 6, 7 and 10 Gurkha Rifles, the 1st Battalion the Duke of Edinburgh's Royal Regiment and 5/7 Royal Australian Rifles, were put through their paces and the overall standard of the platoons was assessed.

The concentration was at Puckapunyal Military Training Area. This is an area of approximately 300 square kilometres with a wide variety of terrain. Very little of the ground was ideally suited to Milan with its maximum range of 1,950 metres, and siting the weapon system occasionally caused a few headaches. It was, however, good country for tanks, as none of the scrub, hills or creeks were serious obstacles for the Leopards. The 1st Armoured Regiment had also had the benefit of two previous concentrations, and proved to be a tricky force to engage successfully.

The work up to the live firing was a three-day dry exercise operating against tanks and APCs across the whole training area, which served to jog a few memories as to the real reason why we were in Australia. Memories successfully jogged, we returned to camp for the final preparation for the exercise.

Following a warning order, platoons set about getting all their equipment in order. Firing posts were recalibrated, air bottles for the thermal imaging sights were recharged, and as much time as possible was spent on the simulator getting the firers up to scratch. As always, there never seemed to be enough time, and pieces of equipment that had been functioning perfectly up to that point became temperamental and refused to work. No problem proved to be insurmountable, however, and with a certain amount of co-operation between units, everyone was ready to deploy on time.

Orders followed and were passed down to the section commanders. A large Mussourian force, equipped along Soviet lines, was advancing on a north-south axis, and all anti-tank platoons from 48 Gurkha Infantry Brigade were to be deployed to meet this threat. Recce elements had been sighted and successfully engaged, and the main body of the enemy was due imminently. Chemical weapons had been used, so we were to deploy in NBC 'high'. This involves wearing nuclear, biological and chemical protective equipment, which is very handy when the weather is cold and wet, but not as pleasant

Soldiers of 6 Gurkha Rifles moving up to the firing point with their Milan anti-tank missile launchers. Both men are in full NBC equipment including respirators, NBC suits, rubber gloves and rubber overboots

when the temperature is in the low 30 degrees centigrade. Despite the nature of this piece of information, it was greeted with the usual cheerful stoicism by the soldiers. The air threat was assessed as low, and we had support from elements of 1st Armoured Regiment and 5/7 Royal Australian Rifles.

Due to various exercise limitations, we would deploy by platoons in sequence to a firing point, where firing posts had already been set up. The targets were representative of the BMP I* and had been fitted with thermal tiles to produce an appropriate heat signature when viewed through MIRA, the thermal-imaging sight fitted to Milan. As well as two 'movers', there were a number of static targets for the tanks to engage, and two machine-gun positions would provide small arms fire during the engagement.

The day of the exercise dawned bright and clear, with the prospect of high temperatures and a very uncomfortable shoot; 6 GR were to be the fifth unit to deploy, so they were virtually guaranteed maximum temperatures and a low sun behind the targets.

Platoons were on standby to move once the previous platoon had deployed. A codeword sent over the radio put us on five minutes' notice to move, and the

(Opposite above) All clear to fire

(Opposite below) A Milan missile at the moment of firing

* A Soviet APC.

168

next one received was the signal to deploy. In NBC 'high' we waited near the vehicles for the first codeword. The carefully applied cam-cream was by now smudged, and the flies and the heat were beginning to get tiresome.

From the camp to the firing point at Bunker Hill the distance was only about seven kilometres, but it seemed to take an inordinately long time. Everyone had been instilled with a sense of urgency, and once we reached the debussing point all the equipment was off and deployed in all-round defence in a matter of minutes. As well as firing posts, the Gurkhas were carrying weighted ammunition tubes, MIRA with its bottles and batteries, radios, personal weapons and webbing, so there was a great deal of equipment to get out of the vehicles.

A quick brief from a member of the Directing Staff got the vehicles out of the area and the firers, No 2s and section commanders to the rear of the position. The dummy ammunition tubes were exchanged for live, and as these were being checked by the firers, smoke grenades were thrown and the NBC state was changed to black. With respirators on, everything is made that much more difficult, and simple drills take longer. Once the ammunition had been checked, everyone sprinted towards the firing point and deployed by detachments into fire trenches.

A Gurkha soldier awaiting his turn to move forward to the firing point

A river crossing in Brunei. The British Army maintains a Gurkha battalion in the Sultanate of Brunei and a garrison headquarters. Limited numbers of British Army personnel pass through for jungle training. Here a river crossing is practised

While the firers were briefed by the Safety Staff, the machine-guns were putting down covering fire from each side of the position on to the static targets. Once the brief was complete, the firers engaged the moving targets one by one using MIRA. The targets were at a range of approximately 1,600 metres and there was a great deal of obscuration from smoke generators and battle simulation produced by plastic explosive charges. Once the engagement had started, the Leopards deployed on to the position and fired their main 120 mm armament and their coaxially-mounted machine-guns. After the No 1 in each position had fired he was 'killed off' by the Safety Supervisor, and the No 2 had to take over to fire the second missile from that firing post. A number of the missiles went low, and hit a bank just in front of the target, while two others just missed to the rear of the target. One missile was a rogue and flew out of control and had to be detached from the firing post. Out of a total of twelve missiles, six good hits were scored on the moving target. When all missiles had been fired, the platoon was given the order to stand by to cease fire, and under cover of smoke from the tanks and machine-gun fire, were withdrawn.

In the very demanding circumstances of the exercise, the Gurkhas' performance was a creditable one. But then, throughout their history, it has never been anything else.

A Leopard I tank from Ist Armoured Regiment moves forward to cover the withdrawal after the live firing

South Georgia Survival Training: The Gordon Highlanders

Major F Philip

A little-known part of the Falklands Garrison is the smaller garrison on South Georgia, a dependency of the Falkland Islands. Here Major Frank Philip of the Gordon Highlanders describes a day in his life on South Georgia.

I left the boot room of Shackleton House, to be greeted by an icy blast of wind on my face. The morning ritual of raising the regimental flag of the Gordon Highlanders was taking place before me. The lanyard squeaked as the duty NCO ran the flag up the mast. Even in the pre-dawn half light, the stag's head motif was plainly visible. Underfoot, what had been rich brown mud the evening before was now frozen hard. The temperature had fallen to minus eight during the night. We were at sea level; I shivered at the thought of two nights at a thousand metres above sea level in snow shelters on the De Geer Glacier.

Slinging my rifle across my chest I reached down for my bergen rucksack. I was pleasantly surprised at the ease with which it swung on to my shoulders – it could only weigh about seventy pounds this week! The previous week's load had been heavier due to extra rations, and more awkward due to the skis that had been attached. Mild weather over the weekend had caused what little low-level snow there had been to disappear, and the lower glaciers to reduce to their bare bones of ice and moraine. There was little point in taking skis this week. We would have to rely on crampons for the steep climb up to the col between the De Geer and Paget glaciers, where we knew there to be suitable snow banks for digging snow shelters.

My garrison of Gordon Highlanders, Royal Engineers, Royal Signallers, Medical Corps personnel and a Royal Marine had been on South Georgia now for about four months, and our tour of duty was nearly complete. We had arrived during the height of the summer and had been generally blessed with good weather. The snows of the antarctic winter had been late to arrive.

Our training had centred around mountain and arctic warfare. The climax of this package was a three-week arctic warfare training course, which would earn a qualification not usually afforded to Army personnel unless they are with units operating in Norway. Our mountain and 'antarctic' warfare package had taken place amid the most spectacular mountain scenery. Glaciers spilled into the sea in every direction, and dramatic mountains rose straight up to a high point of 9,625 feet – Mount Paget. Every clear day, the view from our base at King Edward Point was dominated by this magnificent peak.

Once inside a snow hole, life can be quite cosy providing all the rules are heeded

Despite the difficulties imposed by our total isolation, the South Georgia experience had been unique. We had no telephones and no television, and the BBC World Service was our only form of external contact other than our tele-printer link with the Falkland Islands, 1,300 kilometres to the north-west. Mail was dropped by parachute about every fortnight, and we saw a ship every six weeks. The implications of a serious casualty or a surprise attack were clear to us all. Our doctor was on hand to deal with the former, and demanding training to cope with protracted operations in this harsh environment would cope with the latter possibility. We were the most remote British Army garrison in the world and had to be able to look after ourselves.

When we reached the jetty our Gurkha sappers were already in their immersion suits and life jackets. The extreme cold of the water makes the wearing of immersion suits mandatory. The Gurkhas had only recently arrived on the island, and provided the coxswains and crew for our two Rigid Raider craft and the Gemini inflatable boat. Due to a serviceability problem, the Gemini was standing in for one of the Rigid Raiders. It was slower, but very reliable. There was always competition to ride in the Gemini, which hugged the waves better.

As I struggled into my suit, a look at the end of the jetty reminded me of the unusual visitor we had had a week previously. A sperm whale had entered the cove and had come to the surface five metres from the jetty. One of the men who had been standing there had looked straight into the huge creature's eye. The irony of this close encounter was the backdrop of the derelict whaling station of Grytviken, a kilometre across the cove. Half a century before, whales had been hunted out of this very bay. Whaling has left South Georgia for ever, but it is as much a part of its history as Sir Ernest Shackleton's epic adventure and the Argentine invasion of 1982.

Having organised the men and equipment in the boats and ensured that the weapons were all clipped on to the packs by karabiners, we pulled away from the jetty. The patrol insertion would require two lifts. The round trip, to the head of Moraine Fjord and back, was about twenty kilometres, and it would be two hours before the whole patrol was deployed to a landing site close to where the shattered chaos of the Harker Glacier meets the sea. The bow of the Raider soon rose out of the water. The powerful Suzuki engine was still being run in, and made me wonder what its full potential must be. The wind seemed to be dropping, but out in Cumberland Bay there was a good swell.

The sun was beginning to show above the Szeilasko Ice Cap of the Barff Peninsula across the bay to the east. I had tasked two patrols there earlier in the tour for a total of nine days, reaching as far south as the huge king penguin colony at St Andrew's Bay. The reindeer, introduced by Norwegian whalers, which had been shot at the end of each patrol had long since been eaten. They had been a welcome supplement to garrison rations.

The entrance to Moraine Fjord is barred by a reef. The boat crews knew where the hundred-metre gap was, but the pronounced swell and litter of kelp in the water made this a difficult part of the journey. The Raider fouled its propeller on some kelp and the engine cut out just when we were in the gap. Fortunately it restarted, and we were soon into Moraine Fjord.

As snug as a bug in a rug!

174

The fjord was a mass of 'growlers'. These pieces of floating ice break off the heads of glaciers into the sea, and can present a hazard, although with a man at the bow and a reduced speed they can usually be avoided. The previous week, during a boat recce of suitable landing sites at the head of the fjord, a huge mass of ice had broken into the water with a thunderous crack, causing a large tidal wave. The boats had had to turn into the wave to avoid being swamped. The ice we were encountering at the opposite end of the fjord was possibly from that incident.

The Gemini had worked ahead, and coming off the top of a swell landed with a thump on something hard. The engine screamed as it was clear of the water, and the coxswain quickly shut it down. To the astonishment of all in the boat they had landed high and dry on a growler, which was unusual in that it was of transparent ice instead of being milky, and it was flat and almost sub-surface. The refloating operation involved the peculiar sight of men seemingly walking on water.

Seven kilometres down the fjord we picked our way through particularly dense growlers and landed on a shingle beach which was littered with ice deposited by the tide. We removed our suits and, returning them to the boats, then watched the sapper crews pull away up the fjord again. The sun was up by now. The sky was clear and it seemed we were to be lucky, with another day of good weather.

It had been light for well over an hour by the time the patrol was complete, and we quickly set off up one of the ridges of moraine at the side of the Harker Glacier. The ridge we had chosen to take led steeply upwards towards the De Geer Glacier, which abruptly ends about three hundred metres above sea level. It is heavily crevassed in its lower part, and we climbed high above the glacier and then traversed across the steep and infuriatingly insecure scree slope, to reach a point at which the glacier could easily be joined. We stopped on the very edge of the ice for a rest. Our heavy loads, and the speed with which we had climbed, were telling. Ten minutes' rest and a hot drink would do wonders, though.

The De Geer Glacier flattens out at this point, before rising again to the col above the Paget Glacier which was our objective. The ice cliffs of the inner De Geer Glacier looked down on us from the amphitheatre. The sun had been up for over an hour, and we were treated to the impressive spectacle of a huge serac of ice breaking off and crashing down the vertical two-hundred-metre plunge to the main glacier, where it joined the debris of previous falls and avalanches. We knew we were safe on the opposite side of the glacier, with no such hazard looming above us.

Although we could see no crevasse danger, ahead of us on our chosen route up on the left side of the glacier it did steepen significantly. It was therefore prudent to slip into harnesses and crampons. Still with our weapons across our chests we set off, ice axes in hands, as two ropes of five and one of four.

The middle rope had almost reached the top of the steep section and was on its final zig-zag traverse, when Lance-Corporal Robertson, one of the bigger men on the patrol, through either tiredness or lack of concentration, tripped on his crampon straps and began a sliding fall on hard ice. He immediately dropped the rope coils he was carrying in one hand to get both hands on his axe and roll over, using his body weight, on to the pick, making it bite and arrest his fall. Amid much shouting and clanking of gear the rehearsed drill worked well. All the other men on the rope dived down hard on their axes in case the falling man failed to stop himself. We all looked on soberly as Robertson's flask, in its protective case, slid all the way down to the flat part of the glacier, bouncing over and dancing past inviting crevasses as it went. We would collect it the day after tomorrow on the way down, unless snow obscured it. We had to press on, as much was still to be done before nightfall.

When we reached the col, the sun was beating down hard and many of us had our glacier goggles on to reduce the intense glare and the risk of snow

A snow hole in South Georgia

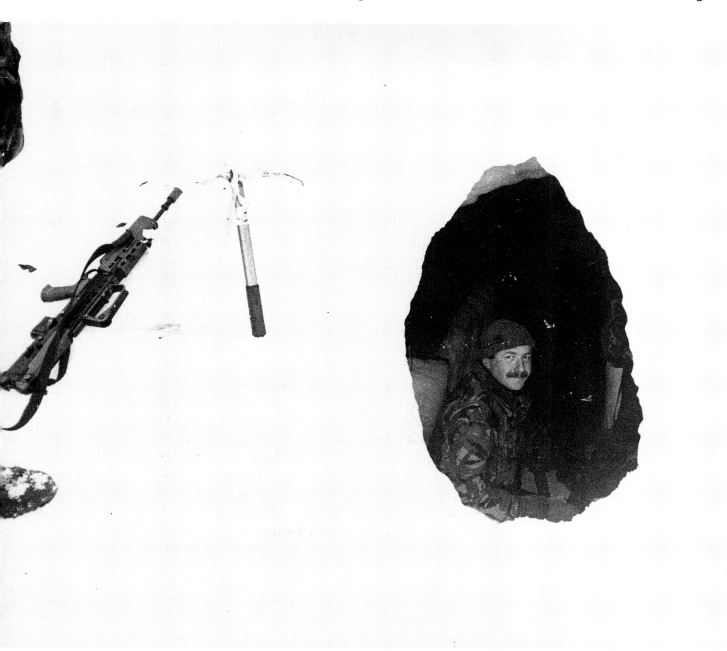

blindness. The snow banks we were to dig into were tested for depth with avalanche probes, and were found to be deep enough. We began work on a selection of two-man snow graves and four- or five-man snow holes. As predicted by the weathermen in the Falklands the night before, a line of cloud could be seen in the distance out to sea. This heralded a front and doubtless some filthy weather, which up here would be even worse.

It was quickly decided that our plans for the following day, a walk across the Paget Glacier, would be affected by the weather. Although ostensibly here to dig and live in snow shelters, we wanted to achieve something more. It was decided to climb the peak on the east side of the col, Point 3452.

Carrying only weapons and webbing we completed the scramble up the rocky ridge and treacherous scree in forty minutes. Some of the men expressed surprise on reaching the summit to find a snow cornice and a long, near vertical, drop on the other side. The view was outstanding. We craned our necks to look at Paget above us and along the jagged white teeth of the Allardyce Range, reaching away twenty-five kilometres to the south. The weather was closing fast, and we descended to the col and recommenced work on our shelters.

Digging in snow is hot, wet work. We stripped off to our thermal underwear and climbed into our Goretex waterproofs for the task. Initially there is only room for one man to dig, while another clears. The further in one digs, the more men can be concurrently involved. Consequently progress is slow to start, but as the snow hole nears completion, progress is made quickly. Outside the naphtha stove was burning constantly. The resting man was in charge of providing a stream of hot drinks to the diggers.

The weather was deteriorating outside, and in the rush to dig in quickly a sweeping stroke from a snow shovel connected with Lance-Corporal Gallacher's knee. It quickly swelled up and later had to be examined by the Medical Officer who was providing medical cover for this patrol.

Three hours after dark we had finished and the business of feeding and organising ourselves for the night took over. The light from the two candles in my snow hole reflected to such a bright extent that it was like being in a well-lit room. Despite the blizzard outside, and the fact that we were in a cave of ice, the temperature was just above zero and remained so all night. With a stove burning the drips increased. It is necessary to keep the roof as smooth as possible to minimise drips, but they always find somewhere to drop off, and an exposed neck is invariably the target. Our water supply was all around us – a mess tin scraped along the roof turned into a steaming brew within minutes. The five men in my hole were soon in sleeping bags, which were themselves inside bivouac bags which provided a waterproof outer layer. The two sleeping platforms were raised above a T-shaped trench, known as the cold well, into which the cold air drops.

Throughout the night a candle sentry in each snow hole lay awake, in case the candles died through lack of oxygen. This can easily happen when snow is being blown around outside and vents are covered. As well as a candle sentry in each hole, a prowling sentry went from hole to hole, checking on the candle sentries and clearing snow from vents and entrances. Everyone, irrespective of rank, would find himself on duty twice in the night.

It had been a memorable day in every respect, with new experiences, some excitement, and challenging problems to overcome. All this had been presided over by breathtaking mountain scenery. All the men with me knew that within a few weeks they would leave the isolated island that had been their home for four months. We knew our South Georgia experiences were unlikely ever to be repeated. For me that is one of the attractions of soldiering – you are always doing or seeing something new. Lance-Corporal Gallacher, whose knee did not prevent him from climbing down the glacier in time for an air-drop of mail two days later, put the De Geer Glacier survival training patrol into perspective:

In one day we practised most of what we had already learnt on South Georgia, and a bit more. I felt privileged to be doing something completely different and I knew there would be nobody back in the Battalion, and certainly none of my civvy mates, who would have done anything similar.

We'd looked south towards Mount Paget for three months but this was our first patrol in that direction. Even a thousand metres up we were still dwarfed by the sheer scale of the peaks above.

I'd never dug a snow hole before. It was perfectly clear to me that teamwork was the key. The same hole could take two or ten hours to dig, depending on how well the jocks supported one another. It was a fantastic day and one I'll never forget.

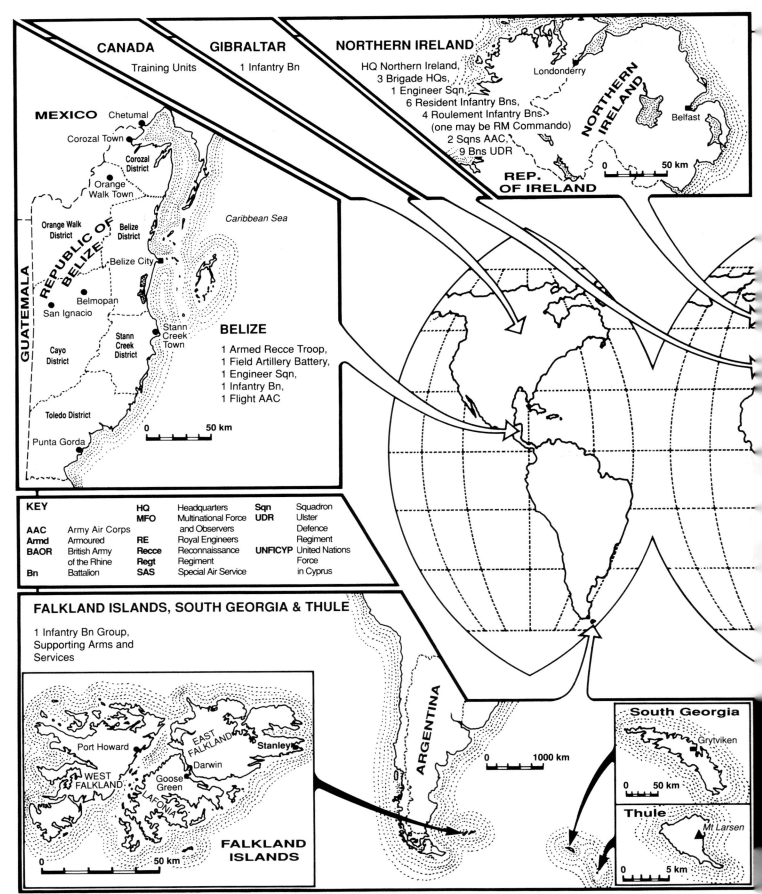

CANADA
Training Units

GIBRALTAR
1 Infantry Bn

NORTHERN IRELAND
HQ Northern Ireland,
3 Brigade HQs,
1 Engineer Sqn,
6 Resident Infantry Bns,
4 Roulement Infantry Bns,
(one may be RM Commando)
2 Sqns AAC,
9 Bns UDR

Londonderry

NORTHERN IRELAND

Belfast

REP. OF IRELAND

0   50 km

MEXICO   Chetumal
Corozal Town
Corozal District

Orange Walk Town

Orange Walk District

Belize District

Belize City

REPUBLIC OF BELIZE

Belmopan
San Ignacio

Cayo District

Stann Creek District

Stann Creek Town

GUATEMALA

Toledo District

Punta Gorda

Caribbean Sea

BELIZE

1 Armed Recce Troop,
1 Field Artillery Battery,
1 Engineer Sqn,
1 Infantry Bn,
1 Flight AAC

0   50 km

KEY

		HQ	Headquarters	**Sqn**	Squadron
		MFO	Multinational Force and Observers	**UDR**	Ulster Defence Regiment
AAC	Army Air Corps				
Armd	Armoured	**RE**	Royal Engineers		
BAOR	British Army of the Rhine	**Recce**	Reconnaissance	**UNFICYP**	United Nations Force in Cyprus
		Regt	Regiment		
Bn	Battalion	**SAS**	Special Air Service		

FALKLAND ISLANDS, SOUTH GEORGIA & THULE

1 Infantry Bn Group,
Supporting Arms and
Services

Port Howard

EAST FALKLAND

Stanley

Darwin

Goose Green

WEST FALKLAND

LAFONIA

FALKLAND ISLANDS

0   50 km

ARGENTINA

0   1000 km

South Georgia

Grytviken

0   50 km

Thule

Mt Larsen

0   5 km

Map drawn by Ethan Danielson

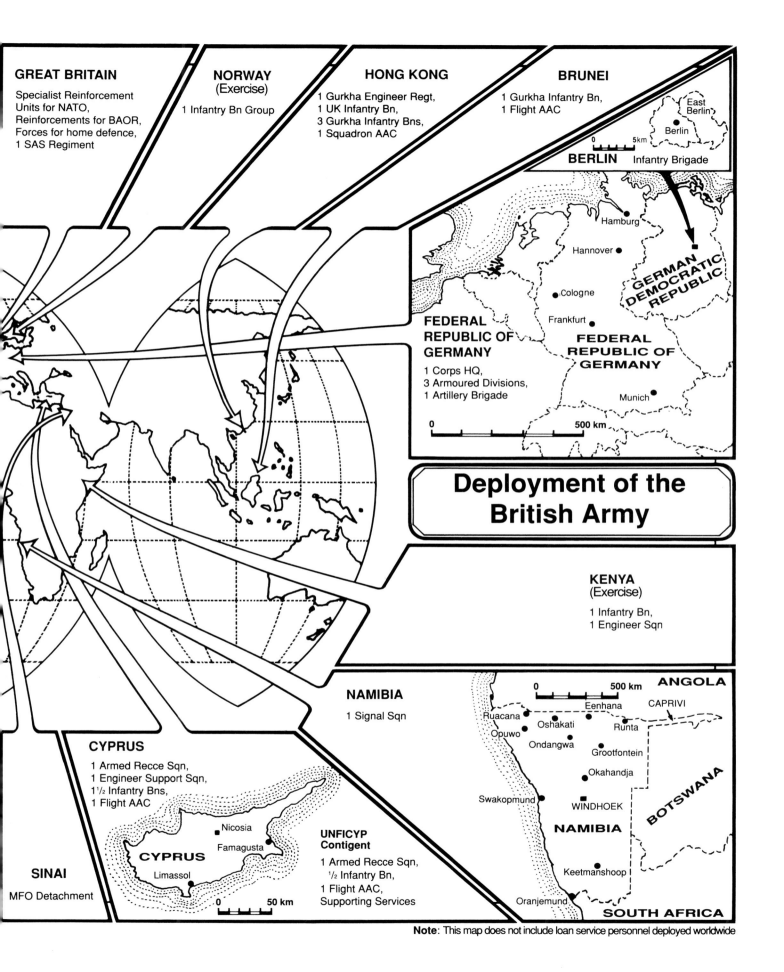

Deployment of the British Army

GREAT BRITAIN

Specialist Reinforcement
Units for NATO,
Reinforcements for BAOR,
Forces for home defence,
1 SAS Regiment

NORWAY
(Exercise)

1 Infantry Bn Group

HONG KONG

1 Gurkha Engineer Regt,
1 UK Infantry Bn,
3 Gurkha Infantry Bns,
1 Squadron AAC

BRUNEI

1 Gurkha Infantry Bn,
1 Flight AAC

BERLIN   Infantry Brigade

East
Berlin
Berlin
0   5km

Hamburg
Hannover
Cologne
Frankfurt
GERMAN DEMOCRATIC REPUBLIC
FEDERAL REPUBLIC OF GERMANY
Munich

FEDERAL REPUBLIC OF GERMANY

1 Corps HQ,
3 Armoured Divisions,
1 Artillery Brigade

0   500 km

KENYA
(Exercise)

1 Infantry Bn,
1 Engineer Sqn

NAMIBIA

1 Signal Sqn

ANGOLA
0   500 km
Ruacana   Eenhana   CAPRIVI
Opuwo   Oshakati   Runta
Ondangwa
Grootfontein
Okahandja
Swakopmund   WINDHOEK
NAMIBIA   BOTSWANA
Keetmanshoop
Oranjemund
SOUTH AFRICA

CYPRUS

1 Armed Recce Sqn,
1 Engineer Support Sqn,
1½ Infantry Bns,
1 Flight AAC

Nicosia
Famagusta
CYPRUS
Limassol
0   50 km

UNFICYP Contigent

1 Armed Recce Sqn,
½ Infantry Bn,
1 Flight AAC,
Supporting Services

SINAI

MFO Detachment

Note: This map does not include loan service personnel deployed worldwide

Conclusion

The thirtieth of June 1989 was chosen at random. Had another day been chosen, the stories would have been different, but equally varied and interesting. The fact is that, though the British Army is a relatively small army, for historical and strategic reasons it finds itself spread all over the world, fulfilling a number of very different and challenging tasks. And it is likely to be asked to continue in this vein for the foreseeable future. Despite the altered situation in Germany and whatever arms reduction talks in Vienna bring – and we all hope they will bring substantial and lasting reductions in manpower and equipment in both the Warsaw Pact and the NATO armies – the British Army of the Rhine is likely to be around for some time to come, though it will be smaller. Moreover, regional instability in other parts of the world shows no signs of abating. Britain will have to maintain forces to look after her residual colonial responsibilities and her other vital interests worldwide. And there will always be a requirement to be ready to defend the British Isles.

The British Army has a long and glorious history. It has amassed a wealth of traditions. It is also a highly professional organisation operating equipment on the frontiers of technology. Clearly the British Army – our Army – is alive and well. And it has every intention of remaining so.

An infantryman on patrol in Belize. He is wearing lightweight combat kit and is armed with a Light Support Weapon

Annex A: Regiments and Corps of the Regular Army

Mounted Troops
The Life Guards
The Blues and Royals
King's Troop, Royal Horse Artillery

Royal Armoured Corps
1st The Queen's Dragoon Guards
The Royal Scots Dragoon Guards
4th/7th Royal Dragoon Guards
5th Royal Inniskilling Dragoon Guards
The Queen's Own Hussars
The Queen's Royal Irish Hussars
9th/12th Royal Lancers (Prince of Wales's)
The Royal Hussars (Prince of Wales's Own)
13th/18th Royal Hussars (Queen Mary's Own)
14th/20th King's Hussars
15th/19th The King's Royal Hussars
16th/5th The Queen's Royal Lancers
17th/21st Lancers
Royal Tank Regiment *Four regiments*

Supporting Arms
The Royal Regiment of Artillery *Twenty-nine regiments, three batteries*
The Corps of Royal Engineers
The Royal Corps of Signals
The Army Air Corps

The Guards Division
Grenadier Guards *Two battalions*
Coldstream Guards *Two battalions*
Scots Guards
Irish Guards
Welsh Guards

The Scottish Division
The Royal Scots (The Royal Regiment)
The Royal Highland Fusiliers (Princess Margaret's Own Glasgow and Ayrshire Regiment)
The King's Own Scottish Borderers
The Black Watch (Royal Highland Regiment)
Queen's Own Highlanders (Seaforth and Camerons)
The Gordon Highlanders
The Argyll and Sutherland Highlanders (Princess Louise's)

The Queen's Division
The Queen's Regiment *Three battalions*
The Royal Regiment of Fusiliers *Three battalions*
The Royal Anglian Regiment *Three battalions*

The King's Division
The King's Own Royal Border Regiment
The King's Regiment
The Prince of Wales's Own Regiment of Yorkshire
The Green Howards
The Royal Irish Rangers *Two battalions*
The Queen's Lancashire Regiment
The Duke of Wellington's Regiment (West Riding)

The Prince of Wales's Division
The Devonshire and Dorset Regiment
The Cheshire Regiment
The Royal Welch Fusiliers
The Royal Regiment of Wales
The Gloucestershire Regiment
The Worcestershire and Sherwood Foresters Regiment
The Royal Hampshire Regiment
The Staffordshire Regiment (The Prince of Wales's)
The Duke of Edinburgh's Royal Regiment (Berkshire and Wiltshire)

The Light Division
The Light Infantry *Three battalions*
The Royal Green Jackets *Three battalions*

Airborne
The Parachute Regiment *Three battalions*
22 Special Air Service Regiment

The Brigade of Gurkhas
2nd King Edward VII's Own Gurkha Rifles (The Sirmoor Rifles) *Two battalions*
6th Queen Elizabeth's Own Gurkha Rifles
7th Duke of Edinburgh's Own Gurkha Rifles
10th Princess Mary's Own Gurkha Rifles
Gurkha Engineers
Gurkha Signals
Gurkha Transport Regiment

Services
Royal Army Chaplains' Department
Royal Corps of Transport
Royal Army Medical Corps
Royal Army Ordnance Corps
Corps of Royal Electrical and Mechanical Engineers
Corps of Royal Military Police
Royal Army Pay Corps
Royal Army Veterinary Corps
Small Arms School Corps

Military Provost Staff Corps
Royal Army Educational Corps
Royal Army Dental Corps
Royal Pioneer Corps
Intelligence Corps
Army Physical Training Corps

Army Catering Corps
General Service Corps
Army Legal Service
Queen Alexandra's Royal Army Nursing Corps
Women's Royal Army Corps

Annex B: Infantry Battalions in the British Army

The Royal Scots (The Royal Regiment) *One battalion*
The Queen's Regiment *Three battalions*
The King's Own Royal Border Regiment *One battalion*
The Royal Regiment of Fusiliers *Three battalions*
The King's Regiment *One battalion*
The Royal Anglian Regiment *Three battalions*
The Devonshire and Dorset Regiment *One battalion*
The Light Infantry *Three battalions*
The Prince of Wales's Own Regiment of Yorkshire *One battalion*
The Green Howards (Alexandra, Princess of Wales's Own Yorkshire Regiment) *One battalion*
The Royal Highland Fusiliers (Princess Margaret's Own Glasgow and Ayrshire Regiment) *One battalion*
The Cheshire Regiment *One battalion*
The Royal Welch Fusiliers *One battalion*
The Royal Regiment of Wales (24th/41st Foot) *One battalion*
The King's Own Scottish Borderers *One battalion*
The Royal Irish Rangers (27th (Inniskilling) 83rd and 87th) *Two battalions*
The Gloucestershire Regiment *One battalion*
The Worcestershire and Sherwood Foresters Regiment (29th/45th Foot) *One battalion*

The Queen's Lancashire Regiment *One battalion*
The Duke of Wellington's Regiment (West Riding) *One battalion*
The Royal Hampshire Regiment *One battalion*
The Staffordshire Regiment (The Prince of Wales's) *One battalion*
The Black Watch (Royal Highland Regiment) *One battalion*
The Duke of Edinburgh's Royal Regiment (Berkshire and Wiltshire) *One battalion*
Queen's Own Highlanders (Seaforth and Camerons) *One battalion*
The Gordon Highlanders *One battalion*
The Argyll and Sutherland Highlanders (Princess Louise's) *One battalion*
The Parachute Regiment *Three battalions*
The Brigade of Gurkhas *Five battalions*
The Royal Green Jackets *Three battalions*

TOTAL:	47 Infantry Battalions
	8 Guards Battalions (not included above)
	—
GRAND TOTAL:	55 Battalions
	—

Annex C: The Territorial Army

Cavalry
The Royal Yeomanry
The Queen's Own Yeomanry
The Royal Wessex Yeomanry
The Queen's Own Mercian Yeomanry
The Duke of Lancaster's Own Yeomanry

Infantry (43 Battalions)
1st Bn The Lowland Volunteers
2nd Bn The Lowland Volunteers
1st Bn The Highland Volunteers
2nd Bn The Highland Volunteers
3rd Bn The Highland Volunteers
5th Bn The Queen's Regiment
6/7th Bn The Queen's Regiment
5th Bn The Royal Regiment of Fusiliers
6th Bn The Royal Regiment of Fusiliers
8th Bn The Queen's Fusiliers
5th Bn The Royal Anglian Regiment
6th Bn The Royal Anglian Regiment
7th Bn The Royal Anglian Regiment
4th Bn The King's Own Border Regiment
4th Bn The Queen's Lancashire Regiment
5/8th Bn The King's Regiment
1st Bn The Yorkshire Volunteers
2nd Bn The Yorkshire Volunteers
3rd Bn The Yorkshire Volunteers
4th Bn The Royal Irish Rangers
5th Bn The Royal Irish Rangers
1st Bn The Mercian Volunteers
2nd Bn The Mercian Volunteers
1st Bn The Yorkshire & Cleveland Volunteers
1st Bn The Wessex Regiment
2nd Bn The Wessex Regiment
3rd Bn The Royal Welch Fusiliers
3rd Bn The Royal Regiment of Wales
4th Bn The Royal Regiment of Wales
3rd Bn The Cheshire Regiment
3rd Bn The Devon & Cornwall Rifle Volunteers
3rd Bn The Worcestershire and Sherwood Foresters
5th Bn The Light Infantry
6th Bn The Light Infantry
7th Bn The Light Infantry
8th Bn The Light Infantry
4th Bn The Royal Green Jackets
5th Bn The Royal Green Jackets
4th Bn The Parachute Regiment
10th Bn The Parachute Regiment

15th Bn The Parachute Regiment
21st Special Air Service Regiment
23rd Special Air Service Regiment

Engineers
Royal Monmouth Royal Engineers
71 Engineer Regiment
72 Engineer Regiment
73 Engineer Regiment
74 Engineer Regiment
75 Engineer Regiment
131 Commando Regiment
105 Plant Squadron
117 Field Support Squadron
143 Plant Squadron
216 Field Squadron (ADR)
218 Field Squadron (ADR)
219 Field Squadron (ADR)
277 Field Squadron (ADR)

Artillery
The Honourable Artillery Company
100 Field Regiment
101 Field Regiment
102 Air Defence Regiment
103 Air Defence Regiment
104 Air Defence Regiment
105 Air Defence Regiment
266 Observation Post Battery
269 Observation Post Battery
307 Observation Post Battery
289 Commando Battery

Signals
31 Signal Regiment
32 Signal Regiment
33 Signal Regiment
34 Signal Regiment
35 Signal Regiment
36 Signal Regiment
37 Signal Regiment
38 Signal Regiment
39 Signal Regiment
40 Signal Regiment
71 Signal Regiment

and numerous TA units of all the services.

Annex D: The Military Hierarchy

Rank	Badge	Command Appointment Example			
General (Gen)	Crown, Star and Crossed Sword with Baton	C in C BAOR/NORTHAG	Captain (Capt)	3 Stars	Squadron/Company Second in Command
Lieutenant-General (Lt-Gen)	Crown & Sword & Baton	Commander 1 (BR) Corps	Lieutenant (Lt) or Second Lieutenant	2 Stars / 1 Star	Troop/Platoon Commander / Troop/Platoon Commander
Major-General (Maj-Gen)	Star & Sword & Baton	Divisional Commander	Warrant Officer First Class (WOI)	Royal Coat of Arms on forearm	Regimental Sergeant Major (RSM)
Brigadier (Brig)	Crown & 3 Stars	Brigade Commander	Warrant Officer Second Class (WO2)	Crown on Forearm	Company Sergeant Major (CSM)
Colonel (Col)	Crown & 2 Stars	Staff or School appointment	Staff Sergeant (Ssgt) or Colour Sergeant (Csgt)	Crown over 3 stripes	Company/Squadron Stores
Lieutenant-Colonel (Lt-Col)	Crown & 1 Star	Battle Group } Comm-Armoured Regiment } ander Infantry Battalion }	Sergeant (Sgt)	3 stripes	Platoon Sergeant
Major (Maj)	Crown	Squadron/Company/Battery Commander	Corporal (Cpl)	2 stripes	Section Commander
			Lance Corporal (Lcpl)	1 Stripe	Section Second in Command

Annex E: Operational Deployments of British Troops, 1945-90

1945-8	Palestine	1956	Bahrain riots
1947	Aden riots		Hong Kong riots
1948-9	Gold Coast riots		Singapore riots
1948-90	British Honduras (Belize)		Suez operations
1948-60	Malaya	1957	British Honduras
1948-51	Eritrea (operations against Shifta terrorists)	1957-9	Muscat and Oman
1950	Singapore (Hartog riots)	1958	Nassau strike
1950-8	Korean War and subsequent deployment		Aden disturbances
1951	Akaba (Moussadeq oil nationalisation)		Jordan/Lebanon intervention
1952-6	Kenya	1959	Gan riots
1958	British Guiana	1960	Jamaica (Rastafarian riots)
1954-90	Cyprus	1960-1	Cameroons
1955	Singapore riots	1961	Kuwait
	Buraimi Oasis operations		Zanzibar

187

1962	British Honduras
	British Guiana
	Brunei
1963	Swaziland
	Zanzibar
1963-6	Borneo
1964	Zanzibar Revolution
	Tanganyika Army Mutiny
	Uganda Army Mutiny
	Kenya Army Mutiny
1964-7	Aden and Radfan
1965	Mauritius
	Bechuanaland
1966	Hong Kong riots
	Das Island
	Seychelles
1967	Hong Kong riots
1968	Bermuda State of Emergency
	Mauritius State of Emergency
1969	Anguilla
	Bermuda

1969-90	Northern Ireland
1970-6	Dhofar
1972	Bomb scare on *Queen Elizabeth 2* in mid-Atlantic and consequent para drop
1979-90	Rhodesia/Zimbabwe
1980	SAS assault on Iranian Embassy
	New Hebrides (Royal Marines)
1982	Falklands War
1983	Beirut
1989	Namibia

This list does not include flood, hurricane and earthquake relief, particularly by the Royal Engineers, in many countries throughout the world, and continuing operations in Hong Kong to prevent the flood of refugees from Communist China, nor does it include several military missions currently engaged in training a number of African armies or the continuing British contribution to the Peace Keeping Force in the Sinai desert.

Index